CONTENTS

56

40

30

ALL-FOR-ONE BLANKET

Easy

MEASUREMENTS

Approx 48"/122cm x 56"/142cm

MATERIALS

Yarn (4)

Bernat® Pop!™, 5oz/140g balls, each approx 280yd/256m (acrylic)

• 6 balls in #84012 Foggy Notion

Hook

• Size I/9 (5.5mm) crochet hook, *or size needed to obtain gauge*

GAUGE

11 sc and 12 rows = 4"/10 cm using size I/9 (5.5mm) hook. *TAKE TIME TO CHECK GAUGE.*

KEY

◯ = chain (ch)

• = slip st (sl st)

T = double crochet (dc)

BLANKET

Ch 32.

1st rnd: (RS) 2 dc in 4th ch from hook. (Ch 1. Skip next 3 ch. 3 dc in next ch) 6 times. Ch 1. Skip next 3 ch. [(3 dc. Ch 3) twice. 3 dc] in last ch. Working along opposite side of foundation ch, (Ch 1. Skip next 3 ch. 3 dc in next ch) 6 times. Ch 1. Skip next 3 ch. (3 dc. Ch 3) twice in last ch. Join with sl st to top of ch 3.

2nd rnd: Sl st in each of first 2 dc and next ch-1 sp. Ch 3. 2 dc in same sp as last sl st. (Ch 1. 3 dc in next ch-1 sp) 6 times. (Ch 1. 3 dc. Ch 3. 3 dc in next ch-3 sp) twice. (Ch 1. 3 dc in next ch-1 sp) 7 times. Ch 1. (3 dc. Ch 3. 3 dc in next ch-3 sp) twice. Ch 1. Join with sl st to top of ch 3.

3rd rnd: Sl st in each of first 2 dc and next ch-1 sp. Ch 3. 2 dc in same sp as last sl st. (Ch 1. 3 dc in next ch-1 sp) 7 times. Ch 1. (3 dc. Ch 3. 3 dc) in next ch-3 sp. Ch 1. 3 dc in next ch-1 sp. Ch 1. (3 dc. Ch 3. 3 dc) in next ch-3 sp. (Ch 1. 3 dc in next ch-1 sp) 8 times. Ch 1. (3 dc. Ch 3. 3 dc) in next ch-3 sp. Ch 1. 3 dc in next ch-1 sp. Ch 1. (3 dc. Ch 3. 3 dc) in next ch-3 sp. Ch 1. 3 dc in next ch-1 sp. Ch 1. Join with sl st to top of ch 3.

Cont in rnds as established, working (Ch 1. 3 dc) in ch-1 sps and (3 dc. Ch 3. 3 dc) in ch-3 corner sps, until blanket measures approx 48"/122cm wide and 56"/142cm long. Fasten off.

FINISHING

Weave in ends. Block blanket to measurements.•

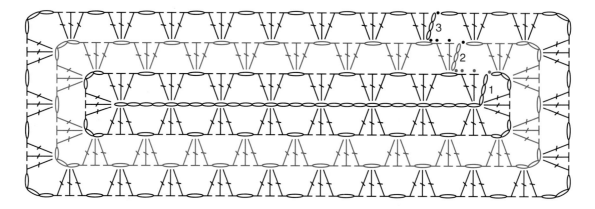

BIG PLAID BLANKET

Easy

MEASUREMENTS

Approx 44"/112cm x 60"/152.5cm

MATERIALS

Yarn (5)

Bernat® *Maker Home Dec*™, 8.8oz/250g balls, each approx 317yd/290m (cotton/nylon)

• 4 balls in #11008 Clay (A)
• 1 ball in #11009 Cream (B)
• 2 balls in #11012 Black (C)
• 2 balls in #11006 Steel Blue (D)

Hook

• Size L/11 (8mm) crochet hook, *or size needed to obtain gauge*

GAUGE

12 sts and 12 rows = 4"/10cm in pat using L/11 (8mm) crochet hook.

TAKE TIME TO CHECK GAUGE.

SIDE PANEL (Make 2)

With A, ch 34.

1st row: (RS) 1 sc in 2nd ch from hook. *Ch 1. Skip next ch. 1 sc in next ch. Rep from * to end of chain. Turn. 33 sts.

2nd row: Ch 1. 1 sc in first sc. *1 sc in next ch-1 sp. Ch 1. Skip next sc. Rep from * to last 2 sts. 1 sc in next ch-1 sp. 1 sc in last sc. Turn.

3rd row: Ch 1. 1 sc in first sc. *Ch 1. Skip next sc. 1 sc in next ch-1 sp. Rep from * to last 2 sts. Ch 1. Skip next sc. 1 sc in last sc. Turn. Rep last 2 rows for pat. Work a further 13 rows in pat. Break A. Join D. **With D, work 16 rows in pat. Break D. Join A. With A, work 16 rows in pat. Break A. Join D.** Rep from ** to ** 4 times more (11 stripes are complete). Fasten off.

CENTER PANEL (Make 1)

Work as for Side Panel, substituting B for D.

NARROW PANEL (Make 2)

With C, ch 16.

1st row: (RS) 1 sc in 2nd ch from hook. *Ch 1. Skip next ch. 1 sc in next ch. Rep from * to end of chain. Turn. 15 sts.

2nd row: Ch 1. 1 sc in first sc. *1 sc in next ch-1 sp. Ch 1. Skip next sc. Rep from * to last 2 sts. 1 sc in next ch-1 sp. 1 sc in last sc. Turn.

3rd row: Ch 1. 1 sc in first sc. *Ch 1. Skip next sc. 1 sc in next ch-1 sp. Rep from * to last 2 sts. Ch 1. Skip next sc. 1 sc in last sc. Turn. Rep last 2 rows for pat. Work a further 13 rows in pat. Break C. Join A. **With A, work 16 rows in pat. Break A. Join C. With C, work 16 rows in pat. Break C. Join A.** Rep from ** to ** 4 times more (11 stripes are complete). Fasten off.

FINISHING

Join Panels tog as follows: Side Panel, Narrow Panel, Center Panel, Narrow Panel, Side Panel, taking care to match stripe/color changes.

Edging

1st rnd: (RS) Join A with sl st in any corner of Blanket. Ch 1. Work sc evenly around outer edge of Blanket, working 3 sc in each corner. Join with sl st to first sc.

2nd rnd: Ch 1. Working from left to right, instead of from right to left as usual, work 1 reverse sc in each sc around. Join with sl st to first sc. Fasten off. •

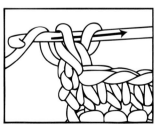
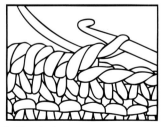

Reverse Single Crochet

CACHE BASKETS

● Beginner

MEASUREMENTS

Small Basket
Approx 11"/28cm diameter x 12"/30.5cm high

Medium Basket
Approx 13½"/34.5cm diameter x 14"/35.5cm high

Large Basket
Approx 15"/38cm diameter x 16"/40.5cm high

MATERIALS

Yarn

Bernat® *Mega Bulky*™ 10½oz/300g balls, each approx 64yd/58m (acrylic)

Small Basket
• 3 balls in #88021 Linen

Medium Basket
• 5 balls in #88609 New Gold

Large Basket
• 6 balls in #88206 Teal

Hook
• Size N/15 (10mm) crochet hook, *or size needed to obtain gauge*

Notion
• Stitch marker

GAUGE

6 sc and 6 rows = 4"/10cm using size N/15 (10mm) hook.
TAKE TIME TO CHECK GAUGE.

BASKET (All Sizes)

Ch 2.

1st rnd: 6 sc in 2nd ch from hook. Join with sl st in first sc.

2nd rnd: Ch 1. 2 sc in each sc around. Join with sl st in first sc. 12 sc.

3rd rnd: Ch 1. *2 sc in next sc. 1 sc in next sc. Rep from * around. Join with sl st in first sc. 18 sc.

4th rnd: Ch 1. *2 sc in next sc. 1 sc in each of next 2 sc. Rep from * around. Join with sl st in first sc. 24 sc.

5th rnd: Ch 1. *2 sc in next sc. 1 sc in each of next 3 sc. Rep from * around. Join with sl st in first sc. 30 sc.

6th rnd: Ch 1. *2 sc in next sc. 1 sc in each of next 4 sc. Rep from * around. Join with sl st in first sc. 36 sc.

7th rnd: Ch 1. *2 sc in next sc. 1 sc in each of next 5 sc. Rep from * around. Join with sl st in first sc. 42 sc.

8th rnd: Ch 1. *2 sc in next sc. 1 sc in each of next 6 sc. Rep from * around. Join with sl st in first sc. 48 sc.

Medium and Large Versions Only

9th rnd: Ch 1. *2 sc in next sc. 1 sc in each of next 7 sc. Rep from * around. Join with sl st in first sc. 54 sc.

10th rnd: Ch 1. *2 sc in next sc. 1 sc in each of next 8 sc. Rep from * around. Join with sl st in first sc. 60 sc.

Large Version Only

11th rnd: Ch 1. *2 sc in next sc. 1 sc in each of next 9 sc. Rep from * around. Join with sl st in first sc. 66 sc.

12th rnd: Ch 1. *2 sc in next sc. 1 sc in each of next 10 sc. Rep from * around. Join with sl st in first sc. 72 sc.

All Versions

Next rnd: Ch 1. Working into back loops only, 1 sc in each sc around. Join with sl st in first sc. Place marker at end of rnd.

Next rnd: Ch 1. Working into both loops, 1 sc in each sc around. Join with sl st in first sc.
Rep last rnd until work from marked rnd measures 10 (12–14)"/25.5 (30.5–35.5)cm. Do not fasten off.

Handles

1st rnd: Ch 1. 1 sc in each of next 9 (12–15) sc. Ch 6. Skip next 6 sc. 1 sc in each of next 18 (24–30) sc. Ch 6. Skip next 6 sc. 1 sc in each of next 9 (12–15) sc. Join with sl st in first sc.

2nd rnd: Ch 1. 1 sc in each of next 9 (12–15) sc. 10 sc in next ch-6 sp. 1 sc in each of next 18 (24–30) sc. 10 sc in next ch-6 sp. 1 sc in each of next 9 (12–15) sc. Join with sl st to first sc.

3rd rnd: Ch 1. 1 sc in each sc around. Join with sl st to first sc. Fasten off. 56 (68–80) sc.●

DECO BLOCKS BLANKET

Beginner

MEASUREMENTS
Approx 46"/117cm x 53"/134.5cm

MATERIALS
Yarn **(4)**

Bernat® *Super Value*™, 7oz/197g balls, each approx
426yd/389m (acrylic)
- 2 balls in #07414 Natural (A)
- 1 ball in #53012 Taupe (B)
- 2 balls in #07483 Walnut (C)
- 1 ball in #08879 Sky (D)
- 2 balls in #53116 Faded Denim (E)

Hook
- Size K/10½ (6.5mm) crochet hook, *or size needed to obtain gauge*

GAUGE
11 sc and 12 rows = 4"/10 cm using size K/10 (6.5mm) hook.
Small motif = 6"/15cm square using size K/10 (6.5mm) hook.
Large motif = 8½"/21.5cm square size K/10 (6.5mm) hook.
TAKE TIME TO CHECK GAUGE.

LARGE MOTIF 1 (Make 8)
With D, ch 4. Join in rnd with sl st to form a ring.

1st rnd: Ch 3 (counts as dc). 2 dc in ring. Ch 2. (3 dc. Ch 2) 3 times in ring. Join with sl st to top of ch 3. Fasten off.

2nd rnd: Join A with sl st to any ch-2 sp. Ch 1. *(1 sc. Ch 2. 1 sc) in same sp as sl st. 1 sc in each dc to next ch-2 sp. Rep from * 3 times more. Join with sl st to first sc. Fasten off.

3rd rnd: Join E with sl st to any ch-2 sp. Ch 3 (counts as dc). (1 dc. Ch 2. 2 dc) in same sp as sl st. *1 dc in each sc to next ch-2 sp. (2 dc. Ch 2. 2 dc) in next ch-2 sp. Rep from * twice more. 1 dc in each sc to end of rnd. Join with sl st to top of ch 3. Fasten off.

4th rnd: With B, as 2nd rnd.

5th rnd: With C, as 3rd rnd.

6th rnd: With A, as 2nd rnd.

7th rnd: With E, as 3rd rnd.

8th rnd: With D, as 2nd rnd.

9th rnd: With A, as 3rd rnd.

LARGE MOTIF 2 (Make 7)
Work 1st to 9th rnds as given for Motif 1, changing colors in the following sequence: B, A, C, D, E, A, C, B, A.

SMALL MOTIF 3 (Make 6)
Work 1st to 6th rnds as given for Motif 1, changing colors in the following sequence: A, E, D, C, B, A.

SMALL MOTIF 4 (Make 6)
Work 1st to 6th rnds as given for Motif 1, changing colors in the following sequence: B, A, E, D, C, A.

SMALL MOTIF 5 (Make 6)
Work 1st to 6th rnds as given for Motif 1, changing colors in the following sequence: C, D, A, B, E, A.

SMALL MOTIF 6 (Make 6)
Work 1st to 6th rnds as given for Motif 1, changing colors in the following sequence: D, A, C, E, B, A.

SMALL MOTIF 7 (Make 4)
Work 1st to 6th rnds as given for Motif 1, changing colors in the following sequence: E, A, B, C, D, A

FINISHING
Following the Assembly Diagram, assemble Motifs as follows:

Joining Motifs
With RS of 2 Motifs tog, join A with sl st in corresponding corner ch-2 sps. Ch 1. 1 sc in same sp as sl st. Working through both thicknesses, 1 sc in each st to next ch-2 sp. Fasten off.

Joining Strips

With RS of 2 Strips tog, join A with sl st in corresponding corner ch-2 sps. Ch 1. 1 sc in same sp. Working through both thicknesses, 1 sc in each st across Strip. Fasten off.

Edging

1st rnd: With RS of work facing, join A with sl st to any corner, work in sc evenly around Blanket, having 3 sc in corners. Join B with sl st to first sc.

2nd rnd: With B, ch 1. [1 sc in each sc to next corner sc. (1 sc. Ch 2. 1 sc) in corner sc] 4 times. Join C with sl st to first sc.

3rd rnd: With C, ch 1. [1 sc in each sc to next corner sc. (1 sc. Ch 2. 1 sc) in corner ch-2 sp] 4. times. Join D with sl st at end of rnd

4th rnd: With D, as 3rd rnd. Join E with sl st at end of rnd.

5th rnd: With E, as 3rd rnd. Fasten off.•

ASSEMBLY DIAGRAM

1	2	1	2	1
5	3	5	4	3	6	7
6	4	7	6	5	4	3
2	1	2	1	2
5	3	5	4	3	6	7
6	4	7	6	5	4	3
1	2	1	2	1

MEGA OTTOMAN

Beginner

MEASUREMENTS

Approx 19"/48cm cube

MATERIALS

Yarn (7)

Bernat® *Mega Bulky*™ 10½oz/300g balls, each approx 64yd/58m (acrylic)

• 10 balls in #88021 Linen

Hook

• Size S (19mm) crochet hook, *or size needed to obtain gauge*

Notions

• Purchased ottoman cube, 19"/48cm

GAUGE

4 sc and 4 rows = 4"/10cm using size S (19mm) hook. *TAKE TIME TO CHECK GAUGE.*

SIDES

Ch 20.

1st row: (RS) 1 sc in 2nd ch from hook and each ch to end of chain. Turn. 19 sc.

2nd row: Ch 1. 1 sc in each sc to end of row. Turn. Rep last row until work from beg measures 73"/191.5cm, ending on a WS row. Fasten off.

TOP/BOTTOM (Make 2)

Ch 20.

Work as given for Sides until work from beg measures 19"/48cm, ending on a WS row. Fasten off.

FINISHING

Sew Bottom to Sides. Insert ottoman cube. Sew Top to Sides.•

HERRINGBONE AFGHAN

Easy

MEASUREMENTS

Approx 49"/124.5cm x 58"/147.5cm

MATERIALS

Yarn (4)

Bernat® *Super Value*™, 7oz/197g balls, each approx
426yd/389m (acrylic)

- 3 balls in #53012 Taupe (A)
- 3 balls in #07414 Natural (B)

Hook

- Size I/9 (5.5mm) crochet hook, *or size needed to
obtain gauge*

GAUGE

13 hdc and 10 rows = 4"/10cm using size I/9 (5.5mm) hook.
TAKE TIME TO CHECK GAUGE.

NOTES

- Turning ch 2 does not count as hdc.
- To join new color, work to last 2 (3) loops on hook
of last st. Draw new color through last 2 (3) loops to
complete st and proceed in new color.

AFGHAN

With A, ch 160.

1st row: (RS) 1 hdc in 3rd ch from hook. 1 hdc in each
ch to end of ch. Turn. 158 hdc.

2nd row: Ch 2. Working in back loops only, 1 hdc in
each hdc across. Turn.

3rd to 7th rows: As 2nd row. Join B at end of last row.

8th row: With B, ch 3 (counts as dc). *Skip next 3 hdc.
1 dtr in next hdc. Working in front of last dtr, 1 dc in
each of 3 skipped hdc. Rep from * to last hdc. 1 dc in
last hdc. Turn.

9th row: Ch 3 (counts as dc). *Skip next 3 dc. 1 dtr in
next dtr. Working behind last dtr, 1 dc in each of
3 skipped dc. Rep from * to last dc. 1 dc in top of
turning ch 3. Turn.

10th row: Ch 3 (counts as dc). *Skip next 3 dc. 1 dtr
in next dtr. Working in front of last dtr, 1 dc in each of
3 skipped dc. Rep from * to last dc. 1 dc in top of
turning ch 3. Turn.

11th row: As 9th row. Join A at end of row.

12th row: With A, ch 2. 1 hdc in each st across. Turn.

13th row: As 2nd row.

Rep 2nd to 13th rows 9 times more, then 2nd to 5th
rows once. **Do not** turn at end of last row.

FINISHING

Edging

Ch 2. Work in hdc down left side of Afghan. Fasten off.
With RS of work facing, join A with sl st to bottom right
corner of Afghan. Ch 2. Work in hdc up right side of
Afghan. Fasten off.•

CUTLERY BASKETS

Beginner

MEASUREMENTS

Small Basket

Approx 6"/15cm wide x 6"/15cm long x 9"/23cm high (unfolded)

Large Basket

Approx 6"/15cm wide x 12"/30.5cm long x 9"/23cm high (unfolded)

MATERIALS

Yarn (5)

Bernat® *Maker Outdoor™*, 8.8oz/250g balls, each 249yd/228m (acrylic/nylon)

Small Basket

• 1 ball in #99003 Summer Storm Gray

Large Basket

• 2 balls in #99003 Summer Storm Gray

Hook

• Size J/10 (6mm) crochet hook, *or size needed to obtain gauge*

Notions

• Stitch markers

GAUGE

11 sc and 12 rows = 4"/10cm using size J/10 (6mm) hook.
TAKE TIME TO CHECK GAUGE.

SMALL BASKET

Ch 2.

1st rnd: 8 sc in 2nd ch from hook. Join with sl st to first sc.

2nd rnd: Ch 1. 3 sc in first sc 1 sc in next sc. *3 sc in next sc. 1 sc in next sc. Rep from * around. Join with sl st to first sc. 16 sc.

3rd rnd: Ch 1. 1 sc in first sc. 3 sc in next sc. *1 sc in each of next 3 sc. 3 sc in next sc. Rep from * twice more. 1 sc in each of next 2 sc. Join with sl st to first sc. 24 sc.

4th rnd: Ch 1. 1 sc in each of first 2 sc. 3 sc in next sc. *1 sc in each of next 5 sc. 3 sc in next sc. Rep from *

twice more. 1 sc in each of next 3 sc. Join with sl st to first sc. 32 sc.

5th rnd: Ch 1. 1 sc in each of first 3 sc. 3 sc in next sc. *1 sc in each of next 7 sc. 3 sc in next sc. Rep from * twice more. 1 sc in each of next 4 sc. Join with sl st to first sc. 40 sc.

6th rnd: Ch 1. 1 sc in each of first 4 sc. 3 sc in next sc. *1 sc in each of next 9 sc. 3 sc in next sc. Rep from * twice more. 1 sc in each of next 5 sc. Join with sl st to first sc. 48 sc.

7th rnd: Ch 1. 1 sc in each of first 5 sc. 3 sc in next sc. *1 sc in each of next 11 sc. 3 sc in next sc. Rep from * twice more. 1 sc in each of next 6 sc. Join with sl st to first sc. 56 sc.

8th rnd: Ch 1. 1 sc in each of first 6 sc. 3 sc in next sc. *1 sc in each of next 13 sc. 3 sc in next sc. Rep from * twice more. 1 sc in each of next 7 sc. Join with sl st to first sc. 64 sc.

9th rnd: Ch 1. 1 sc in each of first 7 sc. 3 sc in next sc. *1 sc in each of next 15 sc. 3 sc in next sc. Rep from * twice more. 1 sc in each of next 8 sc. Join with sl st to first sc. 72 sc

10th rnd: Ch 1. Working in back loops only, 1 sc in each sc around. Join with sl st to first sc. Place marker at end of rnd.

11th rnd: Ch 1. Working in both loops, 1 sc in each sc around. Join with sl st to first sc.

Rep last rnd until work from marker measures approx 9"/23cm. Fasten off. Fold top 3"/7.5cm to outside.

LARGE BASKET

Ch 19.

1st rnd: 1 sc in 2nd ch from hook. 1 sc in each of next 16 ch. 3 sc in last ch. Working across opposite side of foundation ch, 1 sc in each of next 16 sc. 2 sc in last sc. Join with sl st to first sc. 38 sc.

2nd rnd: Ch 1. 2 sc in first sc. 1 sc in each of next 16 sc. 2 sc in each of next 3 sc. 1 sc in each of next 16 sc. 2 sc in each of last 2 sc. Join with sl st to first sc. 44 sc.

3rd rnd: Ch 1. 3 sc in first sc. 1 sc in each of next 18 sc.

3 sc in next sc. 1 sc in each of next 2 sc. 3 sc in next sc. 1 sc in each of next 18 sc. 3 sc in next sc. 1 sc in each of next 2 sc. Join with sl st to first sc. 52 sc.

4th rnd: 1 sc in first sc. 3 sc in next sc. 1 sc in each of next 20 sc. 3 sc in next sc. 1 sc in each of next 4 sc. 3 sc in next sc. 1 sc in each of next 20 sc. 3 sc in next sc. 1 sc in each of next 4 sc. Join with sl st to first sc. 60 sc.

5th rnd: 1 sc in each of first 2 sc. 3 sc in next sc. 1 sc in each of next 22 sc. 3 sc in next sc. 1 sc in each of next 6 sc. 3 sc in next sc. 1 sc in each of next 22 sc. 3 sc in next sc. 1 sc in each of next 4 sc. Join with sl st to first sc. 68 sc.

6th rnd: 1 sc in each of first 3 sc. 3 sc in next sc. 1 sc in each of next 24 sc. 3 sc in next sc. 1 sc in each of next 8 sc. 3 sc in next sc. 1 sc in each of next 24 sc. 3 sc in next sc. 1 sc in each of next 5 sc. Join with sl st to first sc. 76 sc.

7th rnd: 1 sc in each of first 4 sc. 3 sc in next sc. 1 sc in each of next 26 sc. 3 sc in next sc. 1 sc in each of next 10 sc. 3 sc in next sc. 1 sc in each of next 26 sc.

3 sc in next sc. 1 sc in each of next 6 sc. Join with sl st to first sc. 84 sc.

8th rnd: 1 sc in each of first 5 sc. 3 sc in next sc. 1 sc in each of next 28 sc. 3 sc in next sc. 1 sc in each of next 12 sc. 3 sc in next sc. 1 sc in each of next 28 sc. 3 sc in next sc. 1 sc in each of next 7 sc. Join with sl st to first sc. 92 sc.

9th rnd: 1 sc in each of first 6 sc. 3 sc in next sc. 1 sc in each of next 30 sc. 3 sc in next sc. 1 sc in each of next 14 sc. 3 sc in next sc. 1 sc in each of next 30 sc. 3 sc in next sc. 1 sc in each of next 8 sc. Join with sl st to first sc. 100 sc.

10th rnd: Ch 1. Working in back loops only, 1 sc in each sc around. Join with sl st to first sc. Place marker end of rnd.

11th rnd: Ch 1. Working in both loops, 1 sc in each sc around. Join with sl st to first sc.

Rep last rnd until work from marker measures approx 9"/23cm. Fasten off. Fold top 3"/7.5cm to outside.•

EASYGOING BLANKET

Easy

MEASUREMENTS
Approx 48"/122cm x 56"/142cm

MATERIALS
Yarn (7)

Bernat® *Mega Bulky*™ 10½oz/300g balls, each approx 64yd/58m (acrylic)
• 12 balls in #88021 Linen

Hook
• Size S (19mm) crochet hook, *or size needed to obtain gauge*

GAUGE
4 sc and 4 rows = 4"/10cm using size S (19mm) hook.
TAKE TIME TO CHECK GAUGE.

STITCH GLOSSARY
Hdc2tog (Yoh and draw up a loop in next stitch) twice. Yoh and draw through all loops on hook.

NOTE
• Blanket is reversible. There is no RS or WS.

BLANKET
Ch 58.

1st row: 1 sc in 2nd ch from hook. *Ch 1. Skip next ch. 1 sc in next ch. Rep from * to end of chain. Turn. 57 sts.

2nd row: Ch 3 (counts as hdc and ch 1). *Hdc2tog over next ch-1 sp and next sc. Ch 1. Rep from * to end of row. Turn.

3rd row: Ch 1. 1 sc in first hdc2tog. 1 sc in next ch-1 sp. *Ch 1. Skip next hdc2tog. 1 sc in next ch-1 sp. Rep from * across, ending with 1 sc in 2nd ch of turning ch. Turn.

4th row: Ch 2 (counts as hdc). Hdc2tog over first 2 sc. Ch 1. *Hdc2tog over next ch-1 sp and next sc. Ch 1. Rep from * to last 3 sts. Hdc2tog over next ch-1 sp and next sc. 1 hdc in last sc. Turn.

5th row: Ch 1. 1 sc in first hdc. *Ch 1. Skip next hdc2tog. 1 sc in next ch-1 sp. Rep from * to last 2 sts. Ch 1. Skip last hdc2tog. 1 sc in top of turning ch. Turn. Rep 2nd to 5th rows to form pat until work from beg measures approx 56"/142cm, ending on a 3rd or 5th row of pat. Do not fasten off.

FINISHING
Edging rnd: Ch 1. Work 1 rnd of sc evenly around outer edges of Blanket. Join with sl st to first sc. Fasten off.•

BUFFALO PLAID AFGHAN

Designed by MidKnits

Easy

MEASUREMENTS
Approx 52"/132cm x 64"/162.5cm

MATERIALS

Yarn (6)

Bernat® *Blanket Brights™*, 10½oz/300g balls, each approx 220yd/201m (polyester)
• 5 balls in #12001 Race Car Red (A)

Yarn (6)

Bernat® *Blanket™*, 10½oz/300g balls, each approx 220yd/201m (polyester)
• 4 balls in #10040 Coal (B)

Hook
• Size N/15 (10mm) crochet hook, *or size needed to obtain gauge*

GAUGE
6 sc and 7 rows = 4"/10cm using size N/15 (10mm) hook.
TAKE TIME TO CHECK GAUGE.

STITCH GLOSSARY
Splhdc (Split half double crochet) Work hdc between "legs" of stitch (splitting stitch) instead of through top loops.
Surface Sl st Holding working yarn at back of work, insert hook in first ch-1 sp. Draw up a loop. Insert hook into next ch-1 sp. Yoh and pull loop through to front of work and onto hook. Draw loop through loop on hook.

BLANKET
With A, ch 105.
1st row: 1 hdc in 3rd ch from hook. *Ch 1. Skip next ch. 1 hdc in next ch. Rep from * to end of chain. (52 hdc and 51 ch-1 sps). Turn.
2nd row: Ch 1. *1 splhdc in next st. Ch 1. Skip next ch-1 sp. Rep from * to last st. 1 splhdc in last st. Turn. Rep last row 4 times more. Break A. With B, rep 2nd row 6 times. Break B. With A, rep 2nd row 6 times. Break A. Rep last 12 rows for Stripe Pat 8 times more. (114 rows in total have been worked.) Fasten off.

FINISHING
Weave in ends.

Vertical Surface Sl St Rows
Beg with A, working from bottom to top edge, surface sl st in each ch-1 sp of every row. Fasten off. Create vertical stripes by alternating 3 sl st rows with A and 3 sl st rows with B across width of Blanket, as shown in photo.●

COLOR POP BASKETS

Easy

MEASUREMENTS

Small Basket
Approx 7"/18cm diameter x 3"/7.5cm tall

Large Basket
Approx 10"/25.5cm in diameter x 4"/10cm tall

MATERIALS

Yarn **⑤**

Bernat® *Maker Home Dec*™, 8.8oz/250g balls, each
approx 317yd/290m (cotton/nylon)

Small Basket
• 1 ball in #11008 Clay (A)
• 1 ball in #11004 Green Pea (B)

Large Basket
• 1 ball in #11008 Clay (A)
• 1 ball in #11005 Aqua (B)

Hook
• Size G/6 (4mm) crochet hook, *or size needed to obtain gauge*

Notion
• Stitch marker

GAUGE
17 sc and 19 rows = 4"/10cm using size G/6 (4mm) hook.
TAKE TIME TO CHECK GAUGE.

BASKET
Note: Make one Small and one Large. For each, make one with A for Outer and one with B for Inner Basket.
Ch 2.

1st rnd: 8 sc in 2nd ch from hook. Join with sl st to first sc. 8 sc.

2nd rnd: Ch 1. 2 sc in each sc around. Join with sl st to first sc. 16 sc.

3rd rnd: Ch 1. 2 sc in first sc. 1 sc in next sc. *2 sc in next sc. 1 sc in next sc. Rep from * around. Join with sl st to first sc. 24 sc.

4th rnd: Ch 1. 2 sc in first sc. 1 sc in each of next 2 sc. *2 sc in next sc. 1 sc in each of next 2 sc. Rep from * around. Join with sl st to first sc. 32 sc.

5th rnd: Ch 1. 2 sc in first sc. 1 sc in each of next 3 sc. *2 sc in next sc. 1 sc in each of next 3 sc. Rep from * around. Join with sl st to first sc. 40 sc.

6th rnd: Ch 1. 1 sc in first sc. 1 sc in next sc. 2 sc in next sc. *1 sc in each of next 4 sc. 2 sc in next sc. Rep from * to last 2 sc. 1 sc in each of last 2 sc.. Join with sl st to first sc. 48 sc.

7th rnd: Ch 1. 2 sc in first sc. 1 sc in each of next 5 sc. *2 sc in next sc. 1 sc in each of next 5 sc. Rep from * around. Join with sl st to first sc. 56 sc.

8th rnd: Ch 1. 1 sc in first sc. 1 sc in each of next 2 sc. 2 sc in next sc.*1 sc in each of next 6 sc. 2 sc in next sc. Rep from * to last 3 sc. 1 sc in each of last 3 sc. Join with sl st to first sc. 64 sc.

9th rnd: Ch 1. 2 sc in first sc. 1 sc in each of next 7 sc. *2 sc in next sc. 1 sc in each of next 7 sc. Rep from * around. Join with sl st to first sc. 72 sc.

10th rnd: Ch 1. 1 sc in first sc. 1 sc in each of next 3 sc. 2 sc in next sc. *1 sc in each of next 8 sc. 2 sc in next sc. Rep from * to last 4 sc. 1 sc in each of last 4 sc. Join with sl st to first sc. 80 sc.

11th rnd: Ch 1. 2 sc in first sc. 1 sc in each of next 9 sc. *2 sc in next sc. 1 sc in each of next 9 sc. Rep from * around. Join with sl st to first sc. 88 sc.

12th rnd: Ch 1. 1 sc in first sc. 1 sc in each of next 4 sc. 2 sc in next sc. *1 sc in each of next 10 sc. 2 sc in next sc. Rep from * to last 5 sc. 1 sc in each of next 5 sc. Join with sl st to first sc. 96 sc.

Large Version Only

13th rnd: Ch 1. 2 sc in first sc. 1 sc in each of next 11 sc. *2 sc in next sc. 1 sc in each of next 11 sc. Rep from * around. Join with sl st to first sc. 104 sc.

14th rnd: Ch 1.1 sc in first sc. 1 in each of the next 5 sc. 2 sc in next sc. *1 sc in each of next 12 sc. 2 sc in next sc. Rep from * to last 6 sc. 1 sc in each of next 6 sc. Join with sl st to first sc. 112 sc.

15th rnd: Ch 1. 2 sc in first sc. 1 sc in each of next 13 sc. *2 sc in next sc. 1 sc in each of next 13 sc. Rep from * around. Join with sl st to first sc. 120 sc.

16th rnd: Ch 1. 1 sc in first sc. 1 sc in each of next 6 sc. 2 sc in next sc. *1 sc in each of next 14 sc. 2 sc in next sc. Rep from * to last 7 sc. 1 sc in each of next 7 sc. Join with sl st to first sc. 128 sc.

Both Versions
Next rnd: Ch 1. 1 scbl in each sc around. Join with sl st to first sc. Place marker at end of rnd.

Next rnd: Ch 1. 1 sc in each sc around. Join with sl st to first sc.

Rep last rnd until work from marker measures 3 (4)"/7.5 (10)cm]. Fasten off.

FINISHING
Join Outer and Inner Baskets
Place Inner Basket inside Outer Basket with WS facing each other.

1st rnd: Working through both thicknesses, join A with sl st to any st of last rnd. Ch 1. 1 sc in each sc around. Join with sl st to first sc.

Next rnd: Ch 1. Working from left to right, instead of right to left as usual, 1 reverse sc (see page 5) in each sc around. Join with sl st to first sc. Fasten off.•

WAVY GRANNY BLANKET

Easy

MEASUREMENTS

Approx 54"/137cm x 60"/152.5cm

MATERIALS

Yarn **(6)**

Bernat® *Pop! Bulky*™, 9.8oz/280g balls, each approx 147yd/138m (acrylic)

• 5 balls in #93001 Café au Lait

Hook

• Size N/15 (10mm) crochet hook, *or size needed to obtain gauge*

GAUGE

7 sc and 8 rows = 4"/10cm using size N/15 (10mm) hook. *TAKE TIME TO CHECK GAUGE.*

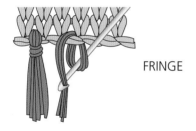

FRINGE

BLANKET

Ch 111.

1st row: (RS) 3 dc in 6th ch from hook (turning ch counts as 1 dc and ch 2 sp). Skip next 2 ch. 3 dc in next ch. Skip next 2 ch. (3 dc. Ch 2. 3 dc) in next ch. (Skip next 2 ch. 3 dc in next ch) twice. *Skip next 5 ch. (3 dc in next ch. Skip next 2 ch) twice. (3 dc. Ch 2. 3 dc) in next ch. (Skip next 2 ch. 3 dc in next ch) twice. Rep from * 4 more times. Skip next 2 ch. 1 dc in last ch. Turn.

2nd row: Ch 3 (counts as dc). (3 dc between 2-dc groups) twice. (3 dc. Ch 2. 3 dc) in next ch-2 sp. *(3 dc between 2-dc groups) twice. Skip next two 2-dc groups. (3 dc between next 2-dc groups) twice. (3 dc. Ch 2. 3 dc) in next ch-2 sp. (3 dc between next 2-dc groups) twice. Rep from * to end of row. 1 dc in top of turning ch. Turn. Rep last row for pat until work from beg measures 60"/152.5cm. Fasten off.

FINISHING

Fringe

Cut 14"/35.5cm lengths of yarn. With 4 strands tog, knot into fringe at points of Blanket. Trim fringe evenly.•

STITCH KEY

⬭ = chain (ch)

T = double crochet (dc)

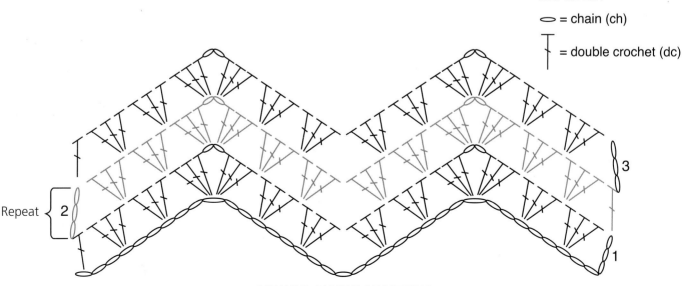

Repeat 2

3

1

REDUCED SAMPLE OF PATTERN

EIGHT SHADES AFGHAN

Easy

MEASUREMENTS

Approx 47½"/120.5cm x 61"/155cm

MATERIALS

Yarn (4)

Bernat® *Super Value*™, 7oz/197g balls, each approx 426yd/389m (acrylic)

- 1 ball in #07438 Baby Pink (A)
- 1 ball in #53022 Dark Heather (B)
- 1 ball in #53531 Rouge (C)
- 1 ball in #07469 Honey (D)
- 1 ball in #53222 Fern (E)
- 1 ball in #53012 Taupe (F)
- 1 ball in #53221 Soft Fern (G)
- 1 ball in #53010 Oatmeal (H)

Hook

- Size I/9 (5.5mm) crochet hook, *or size needed to obtain gauge*

GAUGE

12 dc and 8 rows = 4"/10cm using size I/9 (5.5mm).
TAKE TIME TO CHECK GAUGE.

AFGHAN

With A, ch 272 loosely. (**Note:** Mark every 50th ch with a safety pin to make counting easier).

1st row: (RS) 1 dc in 4th ch from hook. *Skip next 2 ch. (1 dc. Ch 1. 1 dc) in next ch–V-st made. Ch 1. Skip next 2 ch. 1 dc in next ch. Ch 1. Skip next 2 ch. V-st in next ch. Skip next 2 ch. [(1 dc. Ch 1) 3 times. 1 dc] all in next ch. Skip next 2 ch. V-st in next ch. Ch 1. Skip next 2 ch. 1 dc in next ch. Ch 1. Skip next 2 ch. V-st in next ch. Skip next 2 ch.** Yoh and draw up a loop in next ch. Yoh and draw through 2 loops on hook. Skip next 2 ch. Yoh and draw up a loop in next ch. Yoh and draw through 2 loops on hook. Yoh and draw through all loops on hook – counts as cluster. Rep from * to last 25 ch.

Rep from * to ** once. (Yoh and draw up a loop in next ch. Yoh and draw through 2 loops on hook) twice. Yoh and draw through all loops on hook—dc2tog made. Join B. Turn.

2nd row: With B, ch 3. 1 dc in ch-1 sp of next V-st. Skip next dc of same V-st. *V-st in next dc. Ch 1. 1 dc in ch-1 sp of next V-st. Ch 1. V-st in next ch-1 sp. [(1 dc. Ch 1) 3 times. 1 dc] all in next ch-1 sp. V-st in next ch-1 sp. Ch 1. 1 dc in ch-1 sp of next V-st. Ch 1. Skip next dc of same V-st. V st in next dc.** Yoh and draw up a loop in next ch-1 sp. Yoh and draw through 2 loops on hook. Skip next cluster. Yoh and draw up a loop in next ch-1 sp. Yoh and draw through 2 loops on hook. Yoh and draw through all loops on hook– cluster made. Skip next dc of last V-st. Rep from * across, ending at **. Dc2tog over next ch-1 sp and top of turning ch. Join C. Turn. Last row forms pat.

Cont in pat working stripes as follows: 1 row each C, D, E, F, G, H, A, and B. These 8 rows form Stripe Pat. Cont in Stripe Pat until work from beg measures approx 60"/152.5cm, ending with A row of Stripe Pat. Do not fasten off. Work left edging as follows:

Left Edging

1st row: (RS) With A, work sc evenly down side edge of Afghan to foundation ch. Turn.

2nd row: Ch 1. 1 sc in each sc across. Fasten off.

Right Edging

With RS facing, join A with sl st in bottom corner of foundation ch.

1st row: Ch 1. Work sc evenly up side edge of Afghan to top corner. Turn.

2nd row: Ch 1. 1 sc in each sc across. Fasten off.

Fringe

Cut 12"/30.5cm lengths of D and F. Taking 3 strands tog for each fringe, alt D and F for fringe across bottom and top edges of Afghan, working fringe in each ch-2 sp across foundation row or each ch-1 sp across top edge (see illustration on page 18). Trim fringe evenly.●

BOLD ANGLES PILLOW

Intermediate

MEASUREMENTS

Approx 18"/45.5cm square

MATERIALS

Yarn (4)

Bernat(R) *Super Value*™, 7oz/197g balls, each approx 426yd/389m (acrylic)

- 1 ball in #00616 Peacock (A)
- 1 ball in #53223 Grass (B)
- 1 ball in #00607 Berry (C)
- 1 ball in #07711 Navy (D)

Hook

- Size H/8 (5mm) crochet hook, *or size needed to obtain gauge*

Notion

- Pillow form, 18"/46cm square

GAUGE

13 sc and 14 rows = 4"/10cm using size H/8 (5mm) crochet hook.
TAKE TIME TO CHECK GAUGE.

NOTE

- Use separate balls of yarn for each area of color in the design. When joining colors, work to last 2 loops on hook of first color. Draw new color through last 2 loops and proceed.

PILLOW FRONT

With B, ch 58.

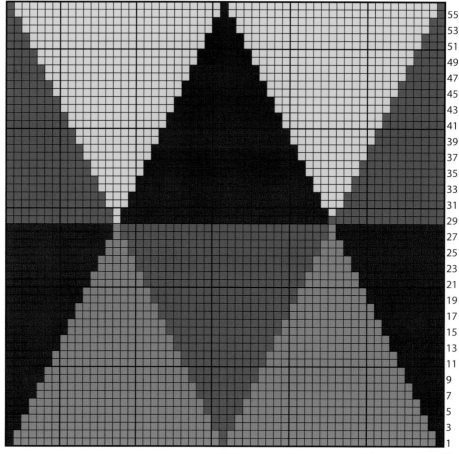

55
53
51
49
47
45
43
41
39
37
35
33
31
29
27
25
23
21
19
17
15
13
11
9
7
5
3
1

Start here

1st row: (RS) 1 sc in 2nd ch from hook. 1 sc in each ch to end of chain. Turn. 57 sc.

2nd row: Ch 1. 1 sc in each sc to end of row. Turn. Work Chart in sc until 56th row of Chart is complete, reading RS rows from right to left and WS rows from left to right and joining A at end of last row.

Next 2 rows: With A, ch 1. 1 sc in each sc to end of row. Turn.

Fasten off at end of last row.

PILLOW BACK

With D, ch 58.

1st row: (RS) 1 sc in 2nd ch from hook. 1 sc in each ch to end of chain. Turn. 57 sc.

2nd row: Ch 1. 1 sc in each sc to end of row. Turn. Rep last row until Back measures same as Front. Fasten off.

FINISHING

Holding WS of Front and Back tog and working through both thicknesses, join D with sl st in corner. Ch 1. Work sc evenly around, having 3 sc in each corner and inserting pillow form before joining 4th side. Join with sl st to first sc. Fasten off.•

HIBERNATE BLANKET

MEASUREMENTS

Approx 52"/132cm x 60"/152.5

MATERIALS

Yarn

Bernat® Blanket™, 10½oz/300g balls, each approx 220yd/201m (polyester)

- 4 balls in #10046 Pale Grey (A)
- 1 ball in #10044 Dark Grey (B)
- 1 ball in #10006 Vintage White (C)

Hook

- Size N/15 (10mm) crochet hook, *or size needed to obtain gauge*

GAUGE

8 sts and 6 rows = 4"/10cm in pat using size N/15 (10mm) hook.

TAKE TIME TO CHECK GAUGE.

BLANKET

With A, ch 106.

1st row: (RS) 1 sc in 2nd ch from hook. *Ch 1. Skip next ch. 1 sc in next ch. Rep from * to end of ch. Turn. 105 sts.

2nd row: Ch 1. 1 sc in first sc. *1 sc in next ch-1 sp. Ch 1. Skip next sc. Rep from * to last 2 sts. 1 sc in next ch-1 sp. 1 sc in last sc. Turn.

3rd row: Ch 1. 1 sc in first sc. *Ch 1. Skip next sc. 1 sc in next ch-1 sp. Rep from * to last 2 sc. Ch 1. Skip next sc. 1 sc in last sc. Turn. Rep last 2 rows for pat.

Cont in pat with A until work from beg measures 10"/25.5cm, ending on a 3rd row. Break A. Join B.

With B, work 10 rows in pat. Break B. Join A.

With A, work 6 rows in pat. Break A. Join C.

With C, work 10 rows in pat. Break C. Join A.

With A, work 6 rows in pat. Break A. Join B.

With B, work 10 rows. Break B. Join A.

With A, cont in pat until work from beg measures 60"/152.5cm. Fasten off.

FINISHING

Side Edging

With RS facing, join A with sl st to bottom right corner. Ch 1. Work 1 row of sc evenly up side of Blanket. Fasten off. Rep for other side.•

HANGING PLANT TRIO

Easy

MEASUREMENTS

To fit plant pots approx 3"/7.5cm in diameter x approx 9"/23cm wide

MATERIALS

Yarn (5)

Bernat® *Maker Home Dec*™, 8.8oz/250g balls, each approx 317yd/290m (cotton/nylon)

• 1 ball in #11012 Black

Hook

• Size J/10 (6mm) crochet hook, *or size needed to obtain gauge*

Notions

• 3 plant pots, approx 3"/7.5cm in diameter
• Dowel, approx 24"/61cm long

GAUGE

12 sc and 13 rows = 4"/10cm using size J/10 (6mm) hook. *TAKE TIME TO CHECK GAUGE.*

FIRST PLANTER

Note: See Diagram on page 28.

Ch 4. Join with sl st to first ch to form ring.

1st rnd: Ch 1. 16 sc in ring. Join with sl st to first sc.

2nd rnd: Ch 1. 1 sc in each of first 3 sc. Ch 2. Skip next sc. *1 sc in each of next 3 sc. Ch 2. Skip next sc. Rep from * around. Join with sl st to first sc.

3rd rnd: Ch 1. 1 sc in each of first 3 sc. Ch 4. *1 sc in each of next 3 sc. Ch 4. Rep from * around. Join with sl st to first sc.

4th rnd: Ch 1. 1 sc in each of first 3 sc. Ch 6. *1 sc in each of next 3 sc. Ch 6. Rep from * around. Join with sl st to first sc. Rep last rnd 7 times more. Do not fasten off.

Hanging Straps

Begin working in rows as follows:

First Strap

1st row: (RS) Ch 1. 1 sc in first sc. 1 sc in each of next 2 sc. Turn. Rep last row until Strap measures 2"/5cm, ending on a WS row. Fasten off.

Second and Third Straps

With RS facing, join yarn with sl st to next sc of last rnd. Work as given for First Strap.

SECOND PLANTER

Make as given for First Planter, working Hanging Straps to measure 3"/7.5cm.

THIRD PLANTER

Make as given for First Planter, working Hanging Straps to measure 4"/10cm.

MOTIFS (Make 3)

Note: See Diagram on page 28.

Ch 4. Join with sl st to first ch to form ring.

1st rnd: Ch 5 (counts as 1 dc and ch 2). (3 dc. Ch 2) 3 times in ring. 2 dc in ring. Join with sl st to 3rd ch of beg ch-5.

2nd rnd: Ch 3. (1 dc. Ch 2. 2 dc) in first ch-1 sp. 1 dc in each of next 3 dc. *(2 dc. Ch 2. 2 dc) in next ch-2 sp. 1 dc in each of next 3 dc. Rep from * around. Join with sl st to top of ch-3. Fasten off.

ASSEMBLY

Sew 3 Straps from each Planter to bottom of each Motif with RS of Motif facing inside of Planter.

Dowel Pocket

With RS facing, join yarn with sl st to first ch-2 sp at top of Motif of First Planter.

1st row: (RS) Ch 1. 1 sc in same sp as last sl st. 1 sc in each of next 7 dc. 1 sc in next ch-2 sp. Working across

HANGING PLANT TRIO

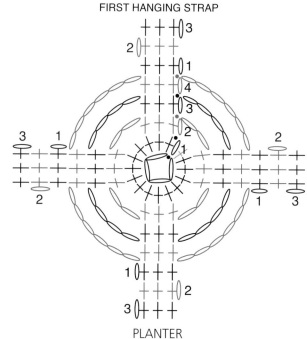

FIRST HANGING STRAP

PLANTER

top of Motif of Second Planter, 1 sc in first ch-1 sp. 1 sc in each of next 7 dc. 1 sc in next ch-2 sp. Working across top of Motif of Third Planter, 1 sc in first ch-1 sp. 1 sc in each of next 7 dc. 1 sc in next ch-2 sp. 27 sc. Turn.

2nd row: Ch 1. 1 sc in each sc to end of row. Turn.

Rep last row until Dowel Pocket measures approx 2"/5cm, ending on a WS row. Fasten off. Sew last row to first row at back of work forming pocket. Insert dowel through Dowel Pocket as seen in picture.

Tassel (make 3)

Wind yarn around a piece of cardboard 5"/12.5cm wide 25 times. Tie through loops securely at one end. Cut across other end. Wrap yarn 6 times around Tassel 1"/2.5cm down from tied end. Fasten securely. Sew one Tassel to bottom of each Planter as seen in picture.●

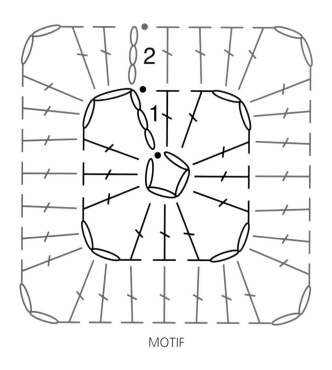

MOTIF

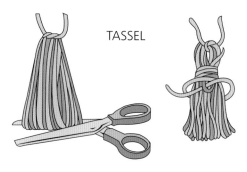

TASSEL

STITCH KEY

◠ = chain (ch)

• = slip stitch (sl st)

+ = single crochet (sc)

╪ = double crochet (dc)

PINSTRIPE BLANKET

Easy

MEASUREMENTS

Approx 52"/132cm x 63"/160cm

MATERIALS

Yarn 6

Bernat® Blanket™, 10½oz/300g balls, each approx 220yd/201m (polyester)

• 5 balls in #10006 Vintage White (A)
• 1 ball in #10044 Dark Gray (B)

Hook

• Size M/13 (9mm) crochet hook, *or size needed to obtain gauge*

GAUGE

8 sts and 6 rows = 4"/10cm in pat using size M/13 hook.
TAKE TIME TO CHECK GAUGE.

STITCH GLOSSARY

Stripe Pat

With A, work 10 rows. With B, work 2 rows. Rep from ** to ** 6 times more. With A, work 10 rows. These 94 rows complete Stripe Pat.

BLANKET

Note: Ch 2 at beg of row does not count as st.
With A, ch 106.

1st row: (RS) 1 sc in 2nd ch from hook. *1 dc in next ch. 1 sc in next ch. Rep from * to end of chain. Turn. 105 sts.

2nd row: Ch 3 (counts as dc). *1 sc in next dc. 1 dc in next sc. Rep from * end of row. Turn.

3rd row: Ch 1. 1 sc in first dc. *1 dc in next sc. 1 sc in next dc.
Rep from *to end of row. Turn.

First 3 rows of Stripe Pat are completed. Rep last 2 rows for pat until 94 rows of Stripe Pat are complete. Fasten off.•

DIP-EDGE BASKET

Easy

MEASUREMENTS

Approx 14"/35.5cm diameter x 9½"/24.5cm high

MATERIALS

Yarn 🄶

Bernat® Blanket™, 10½oz/300g balls, each approx 220yd/201m (polyester)

- 3 balls in #10044 Dark Gray (A)
- 1 ball in #10803 Moss (B)

Hook

- Size M/13 (9mm) crochet hook, *or size needed to obtain gauge*

Notions

- Stitch marker

GAUGE

7 sc and 7 rows = 4"/10cm with 2 strands of yarn held tog using size M/13 (9mm) hook.
TAKE TIME TO CHECK GAUGE.

BASKET

Note: Join all rnds with sl st to first sc.

With 2 strands of A held tog, ch 2.

1st rnd: 8 sc in 2nd ch from hook. Join.

2nd rnd: Ch 1. 2 sc in each sc around. Join. 16 sc.

3rd rnd: Ch 1. *2 sc in next sc. 1 sc in next sc. Rep from * around. Join. 24 sc.

4th rnd: Ch 1. *2 sc in next sc. 1 sc in each of next 2 sc. Rep from * around. Join. 32 sc.

5th rnd: Ch 1. *2 sc in next sc. 1 sc in each of next 3 sc. Rep from * around. Join. 40 sc.

6th rnd: Ch 1. *2 sc in next sc. 1 sc in each of next 4 sc. Rep from * around. Join. 48 sc.

7th rnd: Ch 1. *2 sc in next sc. 1 sc in each of next 5 sc. Rep from * around. Join. 56 sc.

8th rnd: Ch 1. *2 sc in next sc. 1 sc in each of next 6 sc. Rep from * around. Join. 64 sc. Cont in this manner, inc 8 sc evenly around next 5 rnds (as established). 104 sc.

Next rnd: Ch 1. Working into back loops only, 1 sc in each sc around. Join. Place marker at end of rnd.

Next rnd: Ch 1. Working into both loops, 1 sc in each sc around. Join. Rep last rnd until work from marked rnd measures 8"/20.5cm. Join 2 strands of B at end of last rnd. With 2 strands of B held tog, rep last rnd twice more. Do not fasten off.

Handle Openings

Next rnd: Ch 1. 1 sc in each of next 21 sc. Ch 1. Skip next sc. 1 sc in each of next 8 sc. Ch 1. Skip next sc. 1 sc in each of next 42 sc. Ch 1. Skip next sc. 1 sc in each of next 8 sc. Ch 1. Skip next sc. 1 sc in each sc to end of rnd. Join.

Next rnd: Ch 1. 1 sc in each sc and ch-1 sp around. Join.

Next rnd: Ch 1. 1 sc in each sc around. Join. Fasten off.

Handles

With 2 strands of B held tog, ch 26. Thread chain through first ch-1 sp of Handle opening rnd and back out through second ch-1 sp of same rnd. Join with sl st to first ch to form ring, being careful not to twist.

Next rnd: Ch 1. 1 sc in each ch around, rotating chain through Handle opening for ease of working. Join. Fasten off. Rep for second Handle.•

LUMBERJACK THROW

Easy

MEASUREMENTS
Approx 48"/122cm x 63"/160cm

MATERIALS
Yarn

Bernat® *Softee Chunky*™, 3½oz/100g balls, each approx 108yd/99m (acrylic)
- 12 balls in #28044 True Gray (A)
- 4 balls in #28008 Natural (B)
- 1 ball in #28532 Wine (C)

Hook
- Size N/15 (10mm) crochet hook, *or size needed to obtain gauge*

GAUGE
6½ sts and 4½ rows = 4"/10cm in pat using size N/15 (10mm) hook.
TAKE TIME TO CHECK GAUGE.

STITCH GLOSSARY
Dcfp Yoh and draw up a loop around post of indicated stitch, inserting hook from front to back to front. (Yoh and draw through 2 loops on hook) twice.
Dcbp Yoh and draw up a loop around post of next stitch back of work, inserting hook from right to left. (Yoh and draw through 2 loops on hook) twice.

NOTE
- To change color, work to last 2 loops on hook. Draw loop of next color through 2 loops on hook to complete st and proceed in next color.
- Chain 2 at beginning of row counts as stitch.

THROW
With A, ch 83.
1st row: 1 dc in 4th ch from hook (counts as 2 dc).
1 dc in each ch to end of chain. Turn. 81 dc.
2nd row: Ch 2. 1 dcbp around each of next 3 sts. *1 dcfp around next st. 1 dcbp around each of next 3 sts. Rep from * to last st. 1 dcbp around last st. Turn. 3rd row: Ch 2. *1 dcfp around each of next 3 sts. 1 dcbp around next st. Rep from * to last 4 sts. 1 dcfp around each of next 4 sts. Turn.
3rd row: Ch 2. *1 dcfp around each of next 3 sts. 1 dcbp around next st. Rep from * to last 4 sts. 1 dcfp around each of next 4 sts. Turn.
4th to 51st rows: Rep 2nd and 3rd rows 24 times more.
52nd row: As 2nd row. Break A.
53th row: With B, ch 2. *1 dcfp around next st. 1 dcbp around next st. Rep from * to last 2 sts. 1 dcfp around each of last 2 sts. Turn.
54th row: Ch 2. 1 dcbp around next st. *1 dcfp around next st. 1 dcbp around next st. Rep from * to last st. 1 dcbp around last st. Turn.
55th to 64th rows: Rep 53rd and 54th rows 5 times more. Break B.
65th to 68th rows: With C, as 53rd and 54th rows twice more. Break C.
69th to 74th rows: With B, as 53rd and 54th rows 3 times more. Fasten off at end of last row.
Weave in ends.•

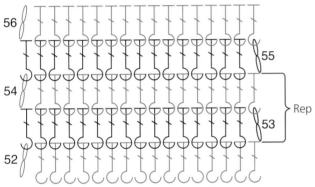

56

54

52

55

Rep

53

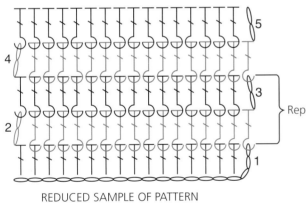

4

2

5

Rep

3

1

REDUCED SAMPLE OF PATTERN

STITCH KEY

⬭ = chain (ch)

┬ = double crochet (dc)

= front post dc (dcfp)

= back post dc (dcbp)

TASSEL & TEXTURE PILLOW

Easy

MEASUREMENTS

Approx 20"/51cm square

MATERIALS

Yarn (6)

Bernat® *Softee Chunky™*, 3½oz/100g balls, each approx 108yd/99m (acrylic)
• 6 balls in #28021 Linen or #28532 Wine or #28048 Taupe Grey

Hook

Size L/11 (8mm) crochet hook, *or size needed to obtain gauge*

Notions

• Stitch markers
• Pillow form, 20"/51cm square

GAUGE

8 hdc and 5 rows = 4"/10cm using size L/11 hook.
TAKE TIME TO CHECK GAUGE.

STITCH GLOSSARY

Hdcfl Half double crochet in front loop only of next stitch.
Hdcbl Half double crochet in back loop only of next stitch.
RSPopcorn 3 dc in indicated stitch. Drop loop from hook. Insert hook from front to back in first dc. Pull dropped loop through.
WSPopcorn 3 dc in indicated stitch. Drop loop from hook. Insert hook from back to front in first dc. Pull dropped loop through.

PILLOW

Ch 42. **Note:** See Diagram.
1st row: (RS) 1 hdc in 3rd ch from hook (skipped ch-2 counts as hdc). 1 hdc in each ch to end of chain. Turn. 41 hdc.
2nd row: Ch 2 (counts as hdc throughout). 1 hdcfl in each st to end of row. Turn.
3rd row (Fringe row): Ch 2. 1 hdcbl in each st to end of row. Place marker at end of row. Turn.
4th row: As 2nd row.
5th row: Ch 2. 1 hdcbl in next st. *RSPopcorn in back loop only of next st. 1 hdcbl in next st. Rep from * to last st. 1 hdcbl in st. Turn.
6th row: Ch 2. 1 hdcfl in each of next 2 sts. *WSPopcorn in front loop only of next st. 1 hdcfl in next st. Rep from * to last 2 sts. 1 hdcfl in each of last 2 sts. Turn.
7th row: As 5th row.
8th row: As 6th row.
9th row: Ch 2. 1 hdcbl in each st to end of row. Turn.
Rep 2nd to 9th rows to form pat. Cont in pat until work from beg measures approx 40"/101.5cm, ending on a 3rd or 7th row. Fasten off.

FINISHING

Fringe

Cut strands of yarn 6"/15cm long. Fold each strand in half and knot into fringe into rem loops of each st

across each marked 3rd row (Fringe row) of pat (see illustration on page 18). Trim fringe evenly.

Assembly
Fold Pillow in half. With WS facing, sew 2 sides of Pillow tog using a flat seam. Insert pillow form. Sew rem seam.●

STITCH KEY

⬭ = chain (ch)

T = half double crochet (hdc)

= popcorn

⌒ = worked in back loop
⌣ = worked in front loop

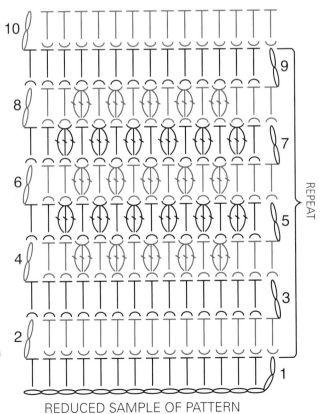

REDUCED SAMPLE OF PATTERN

MIGHTY RIDGE BLANKET

Easy

MEASUREMENTS

Approx 55"/139.5cm x 60"/152.5cm

Yarn (5)

Bernat® *Maker Home Dec*™, 8.8oz/250g balls, each approx 317yd/290m (cotton/nylon)

• 7 balls in #11008 Clay

Hook

• Size L/11 (8mm) crochet hook, *or size needed to obtain gauge*

GAUGE

10 sc and 12 rows = 4"/10 cm using size L/11 (8mm) hook in pat.

TAKE TIME TO CHECK GAUGE.

STITCH GLOSSARY

Scbl Single crochet in back loop only of next stitch.

SQUARE (Make 30)

Ch 2.

1st row: (RS) 3 sc in 2nd ch from hook. Turn.

2nd row: Ch 1. 1 scbl in first sc. 3 scbl in next sc. 1 scbl in last sc. Turn. 5 sc.

3rd row: Ch 1. 1 scbl in each of first 2 sc. 3 scbl in next sc. 1 scbl in each of last 2 sc. Turn. 7 sc.

4th row: Ch 1. 1 scbl in each of first 3 sc. 3 scbl in next sc. 1 scbl in each of last 3 sc. Turn. 9 sc.

5th row: Ch 1. 1 scbl in each of first 4 sc. 3 scbl in next sc. 1 scbl in each of last 4 sc. Turn. 11 sc. Cont in same manner, working 2 sc increases as established each row, until 26 rows in total have been worked. 53 sc. Fasten off.

FINISHING

Sew Squares into 5 Strips, having 6 Squares in each Strip. Sew Strips tog.●

RIPPLES IN THE SAND AFGHAN

Easy

MEASUREMENTS
Approx 56"/142cm x 60"/152.5cm

MATERIALS
Yarn (5)
Bernat® *Maker Home Dec™*, 8.8oz/250g balls, each approx 317yd/290m (cotton/nylon)
• 7 balls in #11008 Clay or #11009 Cream or #11016 Nautical Varg

Hook
• Size L/11 (8mm) crochet hook, *or size needed to obtain gauge*

GAUGE
10 dc and 6 rows = 4"/10cm using size L/11 (8mm) hook.
TAKE TIME TO CHECK GAUGE.

STITCH GLOSSARY
Dc3tog (Yoh and draw up a loop in next stitch. Yoh and draw through 2 loops on hook) 3 times. Yoh and draw through all loops on hook.

AFGHAN
Ch 181.

1st row: (RS) 1 dc in 5th ch from hook (skipped ch-4 counts as 1 dc and ch 1). 1 dc in each of next 8 ch. *(Yoh and draw up a loop in next ch. Yoh and draw through 2 loops on hook. Skip next ch) twice. Yoh and draw up a loop in next ch. Yoh and draw through 2 loops on hook. Yoh and draw through all 4 loops on hook—cluster over next 5 ch made. 1 dc in each of next dc. Ch 3. 1 dc) in next st. 1 dc in 8 ch. (1 each of next 8 ch. Rep from * to last 14 ch. Cluster over next 5 ch. 1 dc in each of next 8 ch. (1 dc. Ch 1. 1 dc) in last ch. Turn.

2nd row: Ch 4 (counts as 1 dc and ch-1). 1 dc in first ch-1 sp. (Ch 1. Skip next dc. 1 dc in next dc) 4 times. *Skip next dc. 1 dc in next st. Skip next dc. (1 dc in next dc. Ch 1. Skip next dc) 4 times. (1 dc. Ch 3. 1 dc) in ch-3 sp. (Ch 1. Skip next dc. 1 dc in next dc) 4 times. Rep from * to last 13 sts. Skip next dc. 1 dc in next dc. Skip next dc. (1 dc in next dc. Ch 1. Skip next dc) 4 times. (1 dc. Ch 1. 1 dc) in turning ch. Turn.

3rd row: Ch 4 (counts as 1 dc and ch-1). 1 dc in each of next 9 sts. *Dc3tog. 1 dc in each of next 8 sts. (1 dc. Ch 3. 1 dc) in next ch-3 sp. 1 dc in each of next 8 sts. Rep from * to last 13 sts. Dc3tog. 1 dc in each of next 8 sts. (1 dc. Ch 1. 1 dc) in 3rd ch of turning ch. Turn.
Rep last 2 rows for pat until work from beg measures approx 60"/152.5cm, ending on a 3rd row. Fasten off.•

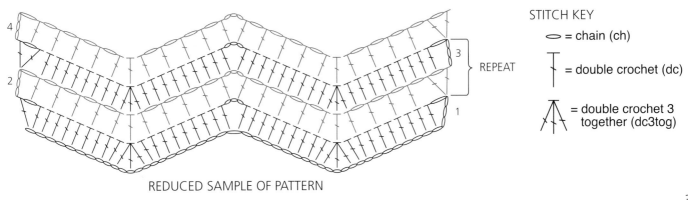

REDUCED SAMPLE OF PATTERN

4

3 } REPEAT

2

1

STITCH KEY

◯ = chain (ch)

𝍐 = double crochet (dc)

⅄ = double crochet 3 together (dc3tog)

PUFFED-UP PILLOW

Easy

MEASUREMENTS
Approx 20"/51cm diameter

MATERIALS
Yarn (5)

Bernat® *Maker Home Dec™*, 8.8oz/250g balls, each approx 317yd/290m (cotton/nylon)
- 1 ball in #11008 Clay (A)
- 1 ball in #11001 Woodberry (B)
- 1 ball in #11009 Cream (C)

Hook
- Size L/11 (8mm) crochet hook, *or size needed to obtain gauge.*

Notion
- Circular pillow form 20"/51cm diameter

GAUGE
5 clusters and 4 rows = 4"/10cm in pat using size L/11 (8mm) hook.
TAKE TIME TO CHECK GAUGE.

STITCH GLOSSARY
Beg Cl (Yoh and draw up a loop. Yoh and draw through 2 loops on hook) 3 times in indicated space. Yoh and draw through all loops on hook.

Cluster (Yoh and draw up a loop. Yoh and draw through 2 loops on hook) 4 times in indicated space. Yoh and draw through all loops on hook.

FRONT/BACK (Make 2)
With A, ch 4. Join with sl st to first ch to form ring. (See Diagram on page 42.)

1st rnd: Ch 1. 8 sc in ring. Join with sl st to first sc.

2nd rnd: Ch 3. Beg Cl in same sp as last sl st. Ch 2. *Cluster in next sc. Ch 2. Rep from * around. Join B with sl st to top of Beg Cl. 8 Clusters.

3rd rnd: With B, ch 3. Beg Cl in same sp as last sl st. Ch 2. *Cluster in next ch-2 sp. Ch 2. Cluster in top of next cluster. Ch 2. Rep from * to last ch-2 sp. Cluster in last ch-2 sp. Ch 2. Join C with sl st to top of Beg Cl. 16 Clusters.

4th rnd: With C, ch 3. Beg Cl in same sp as last sl st. *Ch 2. Cluster in next ch-2 sp. Ch 2. Skip next cluster. Cluster in next ch-2 sp. Ch 2. Cluster in top of next cluster. Rep from * to last 2 ch-2 sps. Ch 2. Cluster in next ch-2 sp. Ch 2. Skip next cluster. Cluster in last ch-2 sp. Ch 2. Join A with sl st to top of Beg Cl. 24 Clusters.

5th rnd: With A, ch 3. Beg Cl in same sp as last sl st. *Ch 2. Cluster in next ch-2 sp. (Ch 2. Skip next cluster. Cluster in next ch-2 sp) twice. Ch 2. Cluster in top of next cluster. Rep from * to last 3 ch-2 sps. Ch 2. Cluster in next ch-2 sp. (Ch 2. Skip next cluster. Cluster in next ch-1 sp) twice. Ch 2. Join B with sl st to top of Beg Cl. 32 Clusters.

6th rnd: With B, ch 3. Beg Cl in same sp as last sl st. *Ch 2. Cluster in next ch-2 sp. (Ch 2. Skip next cluster. Cluster in next ch-2 sp) three times. Ch 2. Cluster in top of next cluster. Rep from * to last 4 ch-2 sps. Ch 2. Cluster in next ch-2 sp. (Ch 2. Skip next cluster. Cluster in next ch-1 sp) three times. Ch 2. Join C with sl st to top of Beg Cl. 40 Clusters.

7th rnd: With C, ch 3. Beg Cl in same sp as last sl st. *Ch 2. Cluster in next ch-2 sp. (Ch 2. Skip next cluster. Cluster in next ch-2 sp) four times. Ch 2. Cluster in top of next cluster. Rep from * to last 5 ch-2 sps. Ch 2. Cluster in next ch-2 sp. (Ch 2. Skip next cluster. Cluster in next ch-2 sp) four times. Ch 2. Join A with sl st to top of Beg Cl. 48 Clusters.

8th rnd: With A, ch 3. Beg Cl in same sp as last sl st. *Ch 2. Cluster in next ch-2 sp. (Ch 2. Skip next cluster. Cluster in next ch-2 sp) five times. Ch 2. Cluster in top of next cluster. Rep from * to last 6 ch-2 sps. Ch 2. Cluster in next ch-2 sp. (Ch 2. Skip next cluster. Cluster in next ch-2 sp) five times. Ch 2. Join B with sl st to top of Beg Cl. 56 Clusters.

9th rnd: With B, ch 3. Beg Cl in same sp as last sl st.

PUFFED-UP PILLOW

*Ch 2. Cluster in next ch-2 sp. (Ch 2. Skip next cluster. Cluster in next ch-2 sp) six times. Ch 2. Cluster in top of next cluster. Rep from * to last 7 ch-2 sps. Ch 2. Cluster in next ch-2 sp. (Ch 2. Skip next cluster. Cluster in next ch-2 sp) six times. Ch 2. Join C, with sl st to top of Beg Cl. 64 Clusters.

10th rnd: With C, ch 3. Beg Cl in same sp as last sl st. *Ch 2. Cluster in next ch-2 sp. (Ch 2. Skip next cluster. Cluster in next ch-2 sp) seven times. Ch 2. Cluster in top of next cluster. Rep from * to last 8 ch-2 sps. Ch 2. Cluster in next ch-1 sp. (Ch 2. Skip next cluster. Cluster in next ch-2 sp) seven times. Ch 2. Join A with sl st to top of Beg Cl. 72 Clusters.

11th rnd: With A, ch 3. Beg Cl in same sp as last sl st. *Ch 2.

Cluster in next ch-2 sp. (Ch 2. Skip next cluster. Cluster in next ch-2 sp) eight times. Ch 2. Cluster in top of next cluster. Rep from * to last 9 ch-2 sps. Ch 2. Cluster in next ch-2 sp. (Ch 2. Skip next cluster. Cluster in next ch-2 sp) eight times. Ch 2. Join with sl st to top of Beg Cl. 80 Clusters. Fasten off.

FINISHING

Join Front and Back

Note: Insert pillow form at halfway point of joining Front and Back.

1st rnd: With WS facing each other, join A with sl st to any ch-2 sp. Working through both thicknesses, work 1 sc in each ch-2 sp and cluster around. Join with sl st to first sc. Fasten off.•

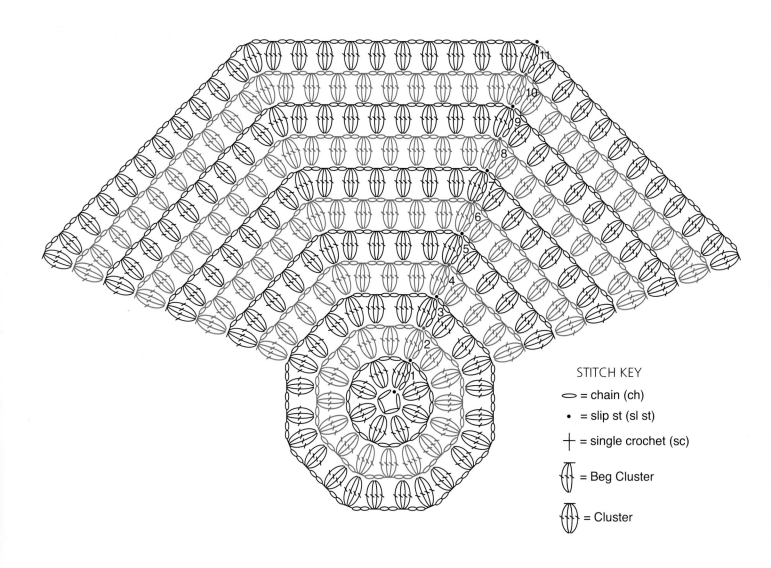

STITCH KEY

◠ = chain (ch)

• = slip st (sl st)

+ = single crochet (sc)

⫶ = Beg Cluster

⫶ = Cluster

PATCHWORK BLANKET

Easy

MEASUREMENTS
Approx 47½"/120.5cm x 50"/127cm

MATERIALS
Yarn ⑥

Bernat® *Softee Chunky*™, 3½oz/100g balls, each approx 108yd/99m (acrylic)
- 6 balls in #28044 True Grey (A)
- 5 balls in #28607 Glowing Gold (B)
- 4 balls in #28047 Grey Ragg (C)

Hook
- Size N/15 (10mm) crochet hook, *or size needed to obtain gauge*

GAUGE
10 sts and 9 rows = 4"/10cm in pat using size N/15 (10mm) hook.
TAKE TIME TO CHECK GAUGE.

NOTES
- Wind balls of the colors to be used, one for each separate area of color in the design.
- To change color, work to last 2 loops on hook and draw new color through last 2 loops and proceed, keeping color change to WS of work.

BLANKET
With A, ch 16. *With B, ch 17. With A, ch 17. Rep from * twice more. With A, ch 2. 120 ch total.

1st row: (RS) With A, 1 sc in 2nd ch from hook. (Ch 1. Skip next ch. 1 sc in next ch) 8 times, joining B in last sc. *With B, 1 sc in next ch. (Ch 1. Skip next ch. 1 sc in next ch) 8 times, joining A in last sc. With A, 1 sc in next ch. (Ch 1. Skip next ch. 1 sc in next ch) 8 times, joining B in last sc. Rep from * twice more. *Do not* join B at end of row. 119 sts. Turn.

2nd row: With A, ch 1. 1 sc in first sc. (1 sc in next

ch-1 sp. Ch 1. Skip next sc) 7 times. 1 sc in next ch-1 sp. 1 sc in next sc, joining B. *With B, 1 sc in next sc. (1 sc in next ch-1 sp. Ch 1. Skip next sc) 7 times. 1 sc in next ch-1 sp. 1 sc in next sc, joining A. With A, 1 sc in next sc. (1 sc in next ch-1 sp. Ch 1. Skip next sc) 7 times. 1 sc in next ch-1 sp. 1 sc in next sc, joining B. Rep from * twice more. *Do not* join B at end of row. Turn.

3rd row: With A, ch 1. 1 sc in first sc. (Ch 1. Skip next sc. 1 sc in next ch-1 sp) 7 times. Ch 1. Skip next sc. 1 sc in next sc, joining B. *With B, 1 sc in next sc. (Ch 1. Skip next sc. 1 sc in next ch-1 sp) 7 times. Ch 1. Skip next sc. 1 sc in next sc, joining A. With A, 1 sc in next sc. (Ch 1.

PATCHWORK BLANKET

Skip next sc. 1 sc in next ch-1 sp) 7 times. Ch 1. Skip next sc. 1 sc in next sc, joining B. Rep from * twice more. *Do not* join B at end of row. Turn.

Rep last 2 rows for pat 7 times more, then rep 2nd row once, joining B at end of last rep.

**Next row: (RS) With B, ch 1. 1 sc in first sc. (Ch 1. Skip next sc. 1 sc in next ch-1 sp) 7 times. Ch 1. Skip next sc. 1 sc in next sc, joining C. *With C, 1 sc in next sc. (Ch 1. Skip next sc. 1 sc in next ch-1 sp) 7 times. Ch 1. Skip next sc. 1 sc in next sc, joining B. With B, 1 sc in next sc. (Ch 1. Skip next sc. 1 sc in next ch-1 sp) 7 times. Ch 1. Skip next sc. 1 sc in next sc, joining C. Rep from * twice more. *Do not* join C at end of row. Turn.

Next row: With B, ch 1. 1 sc in first sc. (1 sc in next ch-1 sp. Ch 1. Skip next sc) 7 times. 1 sc in next ch-1 sp. 1 sc in next sc, joining C. *With C, 1 sc in next sc. (1 sc in next ch-1 sp. Ch 1. Skip next sc) 7 times. 1 sc in next ch-1 sp. 1 sc in next sc, joining B. With B, 1 sc in next sc. (1 sc in next ch-1 sp. Ch 1. Skip next sc) 7 times. 1 sc in next ch-1 sp. 1 sc in next sc, joining C. Rep from * twice more. *Do not* join C at end of row. Turn. Rep last 2 rows for pat 8 times more, joining C at end of last rep.

Next row: (RS) With C, ch 1. 1 sc in first sc. (Ch 1. Skip next sc. 1 sc in next ch1 sp) 7 times. Ch 1. Skip next sc. 1 sc in next sc, joining A. *With A, 1 sc in next sc. (Ch 1. Skip next sc. 1 sc in next ch-1 sp) 7 times. Ch 1. Skip next sc. 1 sc in next sc, joining C. With C, 1 sc in next sc. (Ch 1. Skip next sc. 1 sc in next ch-1 sp) 7 times. Ch 1. Skip next sc. 1 sc in next sc, joining A. Rep from * twice more. *Do not* join A at end of row. Turn.

Next row: With C, ch 1. 1 sc in first sc. (1 sc in next ch-1 sp. Ch 1. Skip next sc) 7 times. 1 sc in next ch-1 sp. 1 sc in next sc, joining A. *With A, 1 sc in next sc. (1 sc in next ch-1 sp. Ch 1. Skip next sc) 7 times. 1 sc in next ch-1 sp. 1 sc in next sc, joining C. With C, 1 sc in next sc. (1 sc in next ch-1 sp. Ch 1. Skip next sc) 7 times. 1 sc in next ch-1 sp. 1 sc in next sc, joining A. Rep from * twice more. *Do not* join A at end of row. Turn.

Rep last 2 rows for pat 8 times more, joining A at end of last rep.

Next row: (RS) With A, ch 1. 1 sc in first sc. (Ch 1. Skip next sc. 1 sc in next ch-1 sp) 7 times. Ch 1. Skip next sc. 1 sc in next sc, joining B. *With B, 1 sc in next sc. (Ch 1. Skip next sc. 1 sc in next ch-1 sp) 7 times. Ch 1. Skip next sc. 1 sc in next sc, joining A. With A, 1 sc in next sc. (Ch 1. Skip next sc. 1 sc in next ch-1 sp) 7 times. Ch 1. Skip next sc. 1 sc in next sc, joining B. Rep from * twice more. *Do not* join B at end of row. Turn.

Next row: With A, ch 1. 1 sc in first sc. (1 sc in next ch-1 sp. Ch 1. Skip next sc) 7 times. 1 sc in next ch-1 sp. 1 sc in next sc, joining B. *With B, 1 sc in next sc. (1 sc in next ch-1 sp. Ch 1. Skip next sc) 7 times. 1 sc in next ch-1 sp. 1 sc in next sc, joining A. With A, 1 sc in next sc. (1 sc in next ch-1 sp. Ch 1. Skip next sc) 7 times. 1 sc in next ch-1 sp. 1 sc in next sc, joining B. Rep from * twice more. *Do not* join B at end of row. Turn.

Rep last 2 rows for pat 8 times more, joining B at end of last rep.**
Rep from ** to ** once more. *Do not* join B. Fasten off.•

GRAPHIC STRIPES POUF

Easy

MEASUREMENTS

Approx 24"/61cm diameter

MATERIALS

Yarn

Bernat® *Softee Chunky*™, 3½oz/100g balls, each approx 108yd/99m (acrylic)

• 5 balls in #28040 Black (A)

• 5 balls in #28005 White (B)

• 1 ball in #28223 Grass (C)

Hook

• Size L/11 (8mm) crochet hook, *or size needed to obtain gauge*

Notions

• Bean bag, approx 24"/61cm diameter

• Stitch marker

GAUGE

7 sc and 8 rows = 4"/10cm using size L/11 (8mm) hook. *TAKE TIME TO CHECK GAUGE.*

STITCH GLOSSARY

Hdc2tog (Yoh and draw up a loop in next stitch) twice. Yoh and draw through all loops on hook.

NOTES

• To join new color, work to last 2 loops on hook. Draw new color through last 2 loops then proceed in new color.

• Ch 2 at beg of rnd does not count as hdc.

COVER

With A, ch 3 loosely.

1st rnd: 8 hdc in 3rd ch from hook. Join with sl st to first hdc. 8 hdc.

2nd rnd: Ch 2. 2 hdc in each hdc around. Join B with sl st to first hdc. 16 hdc.

3rd rnd: With B, ch 2. (2 hdc in next hdc. 1 hdc in next hdc) 8 times. Join with sl st to first hdc. 24 hdc.

4th rnd: Ch 2. (1 hdc in each of next 2 hdc. 2 hdc in next hdc) 8 times. Join A with sl st to first hdc. 32 hdc.

5th rnd: With A, ch 2. (2 hdc in next hdc. 1 hdc in each of next 3 hdc) 8 times. Join with sl st to first hdc. 40 hdc.

6th rnd: Ch 2. (1 hdc in each of next 4 hdc. 2 hdc in next hdc) 8 times. Join B with sl st to first hdc. 48 hdc.

7th rnd: With B, ch 2. (2 hdc in next hdc. 1 hdc in each of next 5 hdc) 8 times. Join with sl st to first hdc. 56 hdc.

8th rnd: Ch 2. (1 hdc in each of next 6 hdc. 2 hdc in next hdc) 8 times. Join A with sl st to first hdc. 64 hdc.

9th rnd: With A, ch 2. (2 hdc in next hdc. 1 hdc in each of next 7 hdc) 8 times. Join with sl st to first hdc. 72 hdc.

10th rnd: Ch 2. (1 hdc in each of next 8 hdc. 2 hdc in next hdc) 8 times. Join B with sl st to first hdc. 80 hdc.

11th rnd: With B, ch 2. (2 hdc in next hdc. 1 hdc in each of next 9 hdc) 8 times. Join with sl st to first hdc. 88 hdc.

12th rnd: Ch 2. (1 hdc in each of next 10 hdc. 2 hdc in next hdc) 8 times. Join C with sl st to first hdc. 96 hdc.

13th rnd: With C, ch 2. (2 hdc in next hdc. 1 hdc in each of next 11 hdc) 8 times. Join with sl st to first hdc. 104 hdc.

14th rnd: Ch 2. 1 hdc in each of next 6 hdc. (2 hdc in next hdc. 1 hdc in each of next 12 hdc) 7 times. 2 hdc in next hdc. 1 hdc in each of next 6 hdc. Join B with sl st to first hdc. 112 hdc.

15th rnd: With B, ch 2. (1 hdc in each of next 13 hdc. 2 hdc in next hdc) 8 times. Join with sl st to first hdc. 120 hdc.

16th rnd: Ch 2. 1 hdc in each of next 7 hdc. (2 hdc in next hdc. 1 hdc in each of next 14 hdc) 7 times. 2 hdc in next hdc. 1 hdc in each of next 7 hdc. Join C with sl st to first hdc. 128 hdc.

17th rnd: With C, ch 2. (1 hdc in each of next 15 hdc. 2 hdc in next hdc) 8 times. Join with sl st to first hdc. 136 hdc.

18th rnd: Ch 2. 1 hdc in each hdc around. Join B with sl st to first hdc. Break C. PM at end of rnd. Rep last rnd, working Stripe Pat: 2 rnds of B, 2 rnds of A, until work from marked rnd measures

19"/48cm. Cont in Stripe Pat as follows:

Next rnd: Ch 2. (1 hdc in each of next 15 hdc. Hdc2tog) 8 times. 128 sts rem.

Next rnd: Ch 2. 1 hdc in each of next 12 hdc. (Hdc2tog. 1 hdc in each of next 14 hdc) 7 times. Hdc2tog. 1 hdc in each of next 12 hdc. 120 sts rem.

Next rnd: Ch 2. (1 hdc in each of next 13 hdc. Hdc2tog) 8 times. 112 sts rem.

Next rnd: Ch 2. 1 hdc in each of next 6 hdc. (Hdc2tog. 1 sts in each of next 12 hdc) 7 times. Hdc2tog. 1 hdc in each of next

6 hdc. 104 hdc rem.

Next rnd: Ch 2. (1 hdc in each of next 11 hdc. Hdc2tog) 8 times. 96 sts rem.

Next rnd: Ch 2. 1 hdc in each of next 5 hdc. (Hdc2tog. 1 hdc in each of next 10 hdc) 7 times. Hdc2tog. 1 hdc in each of next 5 hdc. 88 sts rem. Fasten off.

FINISHING

Insert bean bag. Thread 2 strands of A or B through last rnd. Pull slightly to secure cover on bean bag. Tie securely.•

QUICK & EASY BLANKET

Easy

MEASUREMENTS
Approx 45"/114.5cm x 58"/147.5cm

MATERIALS
Yarn (6)

Bernat® *Softee Chunky*™, 3½oz/100g balls, each approx 108yd/99m (acrylic)
- 8 balls in #28041 Clay (A)
- 4 balls in #28203 Teal (B)

Hook
- Size N/15 (10mm) crochet hook, *or size needed to obtain gauge*

GAUGE
6 sc and 7 rows = 4"/10cm using size N/15 (10mm).
TAKE TIME TO CHECK GAUGE.

BLANKET
With A, ch 56.

1st row: (RS) Sl st in 2nd ch from hook. Sl st in each of next 4 ch. *1 hdc in each of next 5 ch. Sl st in each of next 5 ch. Rep from * 4 times more. Turn.

2nd row: Working in back loops only, sl st in each of next 5 sl st. *1 hdc in each of next 5 hdc. Sl st in each of next 5 sl st. Rep from * 4 times more. Turn.

3rd row: Ch 2 (does not count as hdc). Working in back loops only, 1 hdc in each of next 5 sl st. *Sl st in each of next 5 hdc. 1 hdc in each of next 5 sl st. Rep from *4 times more. Turn.

4th row: Ch 2 (does not count as hdc). Working in back loops only, 1 hdc in each of next 5 hdc. *Sl st in each of next 5 sl st. 1 hdc in each of next 5 hdc. Rep from *4 times more. Turn.

5th row: Working in back loops only, sl st in each of next 5 hdc. *1 hdc in each of next 5 sl st. Sl st in each of next 5 hdc. Rep from *4 times more. Turn.

Rep last 4 rows until work from beg measures 50"/127cm, ending with a 2nd or 4th row. Fasten off.

FINISHING
Edging
With RS facing, join B with sl st at top right corner of Blanket.

1st rnd: Ch 1. (1 sc. Ch 1. 1 sc) in same sp as last sl st (corner). Work 53 sc evenly across top edge. (1 sc. Ch 1. 1 sc) in next st (corner). Work 73 sc evenly down side. (1 sc. Ch 1. 1 sc) in next st (corner). Work 53 sc evenly across bottom edge. (1 sc. Ch 1. 1 sc) in next st (corner). Work 73 sc evenly up side. Join with sl st to first sc.

2nd rnd: Sl st in next ch-1 sp. Ch 1. (1 sc. Ch 1. 1 sc) in same sp as last sl st. Ch 1. Skip next sc. *1 sc in next sc. Ch 1. Skip next sc.* Rep from * to * across to next corner ch-1 sp. **(1 sc . Ch 1. 1 sc) in next ch-1 sp. Ch 1. Rep from * to * across to next corner ch-1 sp. Rep from ** twice more. Join with sl st to first sc.

3rd rnd: Sl st in next ch-1 sp. Ch 1. (1 sc. Ch 1. 1 sc) in same sp as last sl st. Ch 1. Skip next sc. *1 sc in next ch-1 sp. Ch 1. Skip next sc.* Rep from * to * across to next corner ch-1 sp. **(1 sc . Ch 1. 1 sc) in next ch-1 sp. Ch 1. Rep from * to * across to next corner ch-1 sp. Rep from ** twice more. Join with sl st first sc. Rep 3rd rnd until Edging measures 4"/10cm. Fasten off.●

LATTICE POMPOM BLANKET

Intermediate

MEASUREMENTS
Approx 50"/127cm x 60"/152.5cm

MATERIALS
Yarn (4)

Bernat® *Super Value*™, 7oz/197g balls, each approx 426yd/389m (acrylic)
• 7 balls in #53010 Oatmeal

Hook
• Size US I/9 (5.5mm) crochet hook, *or size needed to obtain gauge*

GAUGE
12 sc and 13 rows = 4"/10cm using size US I/9 (5.5mm) hook.
TAKE TIME TO CHECK GAUGE.

STITCH GLOSSARY
Dcfp Yoh and draw up a loop around post of stitch at front of work, inserting hook from right to left. (Yoh and draw through 2 loops on hook) twice.

BLANKET
Ch 192.
Note: See Chart on page 52.
1st row: (RS) 1 sc in 2nd ch from hook and each of next 6 ch. *3 sc in next ch. 1 sc in each of next 7 ch.** Skip next ch. 1 sc in each of next 7 ch. Rep from * 10 times more, then from * to ** once. Turn.
2nd, 4th, 6th, and 8th rows: Ch 1. 1 sc in first sc. Skip next sc. 1 sc in each of next 6 sts. *3 sc in next sc. 1 sc in each of next 7 sts. Skip next 2 sc. 1 sc in each of next 7 sts. Rep from * to last 9 sts. 3 sc in next sc. 1 sc in each of next 6 sts. Skip next sc. 1 sc in last sc. Turn.
3rd row: Ch 1. 1 sc in first sc. Skip next sc. 1 sc in each of next 5 sc. *Dcfp around next sc 1 row below. Skip next sc behind st just made. 3 sc in next sc. Dcfp around next sc 1 row below. Skip next sc behind st just made. * 1 sc in each of next 6 sc. Skip next 2 sc. 1 sc in each of next 6 sc. Rep from * 10 times more, then from * to ** once. 1 sc in each of next 5 sc. Skip next sc. 1 sc in last sc. Turn.
5th row: Ch 1. 1 sc in first sc. Skip next sc. 1 sc in each of next 3 sc. *Dcfp around next dcfp 2 rows below. Skip next sc behind st just made. 1 sc in each of next 2 sc. 3 sc in next sc. 1 sc ion each of next 2 sc. Dcfp around next dcfp 2 rows below. Skip next sc behind st just made.** 1 sc in each of next 4 sc. Skip next 2 sc. 1 sc in each of next 4 sc. Rep from * 10 times more, then from * to ** once. 1 sc in each of next 3 sc. Skip next sc. 1 sc in last sc. Turn.
7th row: Ch 1. 1 sc in first sc. Skip next sc. 1 sc in next sc. *Dcfp around next dcfp 2 rows below. Skip next sc behind st just made. 1 sc in each of next 4 sc. 3 sc in next sc. 1 sc in each of next 2 sc. Dcfp around next dcfp 2 rows below. Skip next sc behind st just made.** 1 sc in each of next 4 sc. Skip next 2 sc. 1 sc in each of next 4 sc. Rep from * 10 times more, then from * to ** once. 1 sc in each of next 3 sc. Skip next sc. 1 sc in last sc. Turn.
9th row: Ch 1. *Dcfp around next dcfp 2 rows below. Skip next sc behind st just made. Working in back loops only, 1 sc in each of next 6 sc. 3 sc in next sc. 1 sc in each of next 6 sc. Dcfp around next dcfp 2 rows below. Skip next sc behind st just made.** Skip next 2 sc. Rep from * 10 times more, then from * to ** once. Turn.
10th row: Ch 1. Working in back loops only, 1 sc in first st. Skip next st. 1 sc in each of next 6 sts. *3 sc in next sc. 1 sc in each of next 7 sts. Skip next 2 sc. 1 sc in each of next 7 sts. Rep from * to last 9 sts. 3 sc in next sc. 1 sc in each of next 6 sts. Skip next sc. 1 sc in last sc. Turn. Rep 3rd to 10th rows 14 times more, then rep 3rd to 9th rows once. Fasten off.

50

LATTICE POMPOM BLANKET

FINISHING

Pompom (Make 48)

Wind yarn around 2 fingers 50 times. Tie tightly in the middle and leave a long end for attaching to Blanket. Cut loops at both ends and trim to form pompom. Sew pompoms as shown at right. •

DIAGRAM

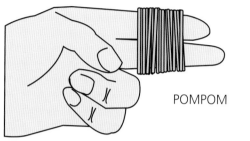

POMPOM

STITCH KEY

⬯ = chain (ch)

✛ = single crochet (sc)

⊥ = Dcfp

⌒ = worked in back loop only

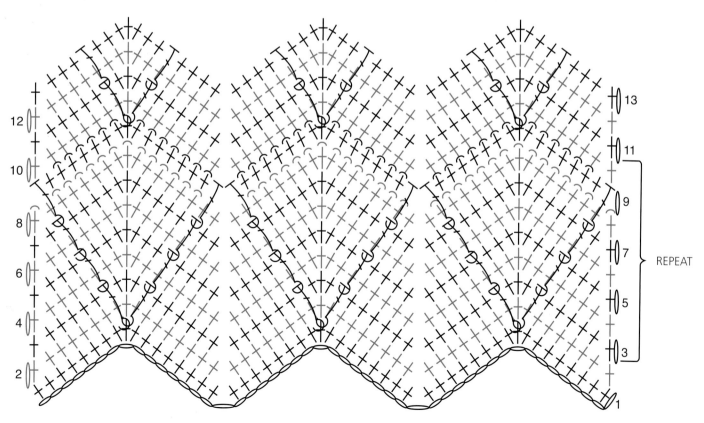

REDUCED SAMPLE OF PATTERN

HANDY BASKET

Easy

MEASUREMENTS

Approx 10"/25.5cm diameter x 10"/25.5cm tall

MATERIALS

Yarn (5)

Bernat® *Maker Home Dec*™, 8.8oz/250g balls, each approx 317yd/290m (cotton/nylon)

- 1 ball in #11006 Steel Blue (A)
- 1 ball in #11008 Clay (B)
- 1 ball in #11009 Cream (C)

Hook

- Size G/6 (4mm) crochet hook, *or size needed to obtain gauge*

Notions

- 1 stitch marker.

GAUGE

17 sc and 19 rows = 4"/10cm using size G/6 (4mm) hook.
TAKE TIME TO CHECK GAUGE.

NOTE

Join all rnds with sl st to first sc.

BASKET

With A, ch 2.

1st rnd: 8 sc in 2nd ch from hook. Join. 8 sc.

2nd rnd: Ch 1. 2 sc in each sc around. Join. 16 sc.

3rd rnd: Ch 1. *2 sc in next sc. 1 sc in next sc. Rep from * around. Join. 24 sc.

4th rnd: Ch 1. *2 sc in next sc. 1 sc in each of next 2 sc. Rep from * around. Join. 32 sc.

5th rnd: Ch 1. *2 sc in next sc. 1 sc in each of next 3 sc. Rep from * around. Join. 40 sc.

6th rnd: Ch 1. *2 sc in next sc. 1 sc in each of next 4 sc. Rep from * around. Join. 48 sc. Cont as established, work 8 incs on every rnd, evenly spaced, until there are 144 sc. (18 rnds are complete.)

Next rnd: Ch 1. Working in back loops only, 1 sc in each sc around. Join with sl st to first sc. PM at end of last rnd.

Next rnd: Ch 1. Working in both loops, 1 sc in each sc around. Join with sl st to first sc. Rep last rnd until work from marked rnd measures 3"/7.5cm. Join B at end of last rnd. Break A.

With B, rep last rnd until work from marked rnd measures 6"/15cm.

Join C at end of last rnd. Break B.

With C, rep last rnd until work from marked rnd measures 9½"/24cm.

Next rnd: Ch 1. 1 sc in each of next 29 sc. Ch 14. Skip next 14 sc. 1 sc in each of next 58 sc. Ch 14. Skip next 14 sc. 1 sc in each of next 29 sc. Join with sl st to first sc.

Next rnd: Ch 1. 1 sc in each of next 29 sc. 17 sc in next ch-14 sp. 1 sc in each of next 58 sc. 17 sc in next ch-12 sp. 1 sc in each of next 29 sc. Join.

Next 2 rnds: Ch 1. 1 sc in each sc around. Join. Fasten off at end of 2nd rnd.•

ZIGZAG AFGHAN

Easy

MEASUREMENTS
Approx 46"/117cm x 58"/147.5cm

MATERIALS

Yarn (4)
Bernat® *Super Value*™, 7oz/197g balls, each approx 426yd/389m (acrylic)

2 balls in #53522 Redwood Heather (A)

2 balls in #53436 Cherry Red (B)

2 balls in #53010 Oatmeal (C)

3 balls in #53222 Fern (D)

Hooks
Size I/9 (5.5mm) and J/10 (6mm) crochet hooks, *or sizes needed to obtain gauge*

GAUGE
12 sc and 13 rows = 4"/10cm using size I/9 (5.5mm) hook. *TAKE TIME TO CHECK GAUGE.*

NOTE
First and last sc of each row is left unworked.

AFGHAN
With smaller hook and A, ch 225. Mark every 50th ch for easier counting.

1st row: (RS) 1 sc in 2nd ch from hook. *1 sc in each of next 9 ch. Ch 2. 1 sc in each of next 10 ch. Skip next 2 ch. 1 sc in each of next 5 ch. Ch 2. 1 sc in each of next 5 ch. Skip next 2 ch. 1 sc in next ch. Rep from * to last 19 ch. 1 sc in each of next 9 ch. Ch 2. 1 sc in each of next 10 ch. Fasten off. Turn. 224 sts.

**2nd row: Skip first sc. Join B with sl st to back loop of next sc. Ch 1. Working in *back loops only* 1 sc in same sp as sl st. 1 sc in each of next 8 sc. (1 sc. Ch 2. 1 sc) in next ch-2 sp. 1 sc in each of next 9 sc. *Skip next 2 sc. 1 sc in each of next 4 sts. (1 sc. Ch 2. 1 sc) in next ch-2 sp. 1 sc in each of the next 4 sts. Skip next 2 sc. 1 sc in each of next 9 sts. (1 sc. Ch 2. 1 sc) in next ch-2 sp. 1 sc in each of next 9 sc. Rep from * to last sc. Turn.

3rd and 4th rows: Sl st in first 2 sc. Ch 1. Working in *back loops only* 1 sc in same sp as last sl st. 1 sc in each of next 8 sc. (1 sc. Ch 2. 1 sc) in next ch-2 sp. 1 sc in each of next 9 sc. *Skip next 2 sc. 1 sc in each of next 4 sts. (1 sc. Ch 2. 1 sc) in next ch-2 sp. 1 sc in each of next 4 sts. Skip next 2 sc. 1 sc in each of next 9 sts. (1 sc. Ch 2. 1 sc) in next ch-2 sp. 1 sc in each of next 9 sc. Rep from * to last sc. Leave last sc unworked. Turn. Fasten off at end of 4th row.

5th row: With C, as 2nd row.

6th to 9th rows: With C, as 3rd row 4 times. Fasten off at end of 9th row.

10th row: With D, as 2nd row.

11th to 18th rows: With D, as 3rd row 8 times. Fasten off at end of 18th row.

19th row: With A, as 2nd row.

** Rep from ** to ** for Flame Pat 7 times more, omitting last row with A at last rep.

Edging
With RS facing and larger hook, join C with sl st to first sc on RS of Afghan. Ch 1. *1 sc in side of next sc. Rep from * along side of Afghan. Fasten off. Rep for other side.●

SNOWFLAKE BLANKET

Intermediate

MEASUREMENTS

Approx 52½"/133.5cm x 63"/160cm

MATERIALS

Yarn (4)

Bernat® Super Value™, 7oz/197g balls, each approx 426yd/389m (acrylic)

• 5 balls in #53042 Dark Gray (A)

Yarn (4)

Bernat® Pop!™, 5oz/140g balls, each approx 280yd/256m (acrylic)

• 5 balls in #84005 Planetary (B)

Hook

• Size H/8 (5mm) crochet hook, *or size needed to obtain gauge*

GAUGE

13 dc and 6½ rows = 4"/10cm using size H/8 (5mm) hook.

TAKE TIME TO CHECK GAUGE.

MOTIF (Make 30)

Note: Ch 3 at beg of rows counts as dc.

With A, ch 36.

Work Chart, noting each square of chart is equal to 2 dc and reading RS rows from right to left and WS rows from left to right. Carry color not in use across top of entire previous row and work sts around it. This will ensure even gauge as all sts will be worked around an extra strand of yarn held across top of previous row. Carry both colors up side of work.

1st row: (RS) 1 dc in 4th ch from hook. 1 dc in each ch to end of ch. Turn. 34 dc.

2nd row: Ch 3. 1 dc in each dc to end of row. Turn.

Rep 2nd row and cont working Chart until 17th row of chart is complete. Fasten off.

FINISHING

Assembly

With A, work 1 row of sc through front loops only to join Motifs tog. Join into 5 Strips, having 6 Motifs in each Strip. Work 1 row of sc through front loops only to join Strips tog.

Border

With RS facing, join A with sl st to any corner.

1st rnd: Ch 3 (counts as dc). Work dc evenly around outer edge, working 5 dc in each corner. Join with sl st to top of ch 3. Fasten off.•

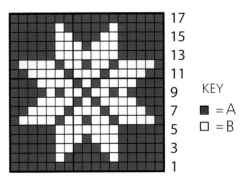

KEY
■ = A
□ = B

Note: Each square in chart is equal to 2 dc.

RIDGE-STITCH POUF

Easy

MEASUREMENTS

Approx 20"/51cm in diameter x 12"/30.5cm high

MATERIALS

Yarn 🔟

Bernat® *Maker Big*™, 8.8oz/250g balls, each approx 77yd/70m (cotton/nylon)

• 4 balls in #25015 Dusk Blue or #25005 Tar or #25011 Chartreuse

Hook

• Size Q (16mm) crochet hook, *or size needed to obtain gauge*

Notion

• Purchased round ottoman, approx 20"/51cm diameter x 12"/30.5 cm high

GAUGE

5 sc and 5 rows = 4"/10 cm using size Q (16mm) hook. *TAKE TIME TO CHECK GAUGE.*

STITCH GLOSSARY

Hdcfp Yoh and draw up a loop around post of next st at front of work, inserting hook from right to left. Yoh and draw through all loops on hook

Hdc2tog (Yoh and draw up a loop in next stitch) twice. Yoh and draw through all loops on hook.

NOTE

• Ch 2 counts as hdc throughout.

POUF

Ch 3.

1st rnd: 9 hdc in 3rd ch from hook (skipped ch-2 counts as hdc). Join with sl st to Join with sl st to top of ch 2. 10 hdc

2nd rnd: Ch 2. 1 hdc in same sp as last sl st. (counts as 2 hdc). *2 hdc in each hdc around. Join with sl st to first sc. Join with sl st to top of ch-2. 20 sc.

3rd rnd: Ch 2. 1 hdc in same sp as last sl st. 1 hdcfp around next hdc. *2 hdc in next hdc. 1 hdcfp around next hdc. Rep from * around. Join with sl st to top of ch 2. 30 sts.

4th rnd: Ch 2. 1 hdc in same sp as last sl st. 1 hdc in next hdc. 1 hdcfp around next hdcfp. *2 hdc in next hdc.1 hdc in each of next hdc. 1 hdcfp around next hdcfp. Rep from * around. Join with sl st to top of ch 2. 40 sts.

5th rnd: Ch 2. 1 hdc in same sp as last sl st. 1 hdc in each of next 2 hdc. 1 hdcfp around next hdcfp. *2 hdc in next hdc.1 hdc in each of next 2 hdc. 1 hdcfp around next hdcfp. Rep from * around. Join with sl st to top of ch 2. 50 sts.

6th rnd: Ch 2. 1 hdc in same sp as last sl st. 1 hdc in each of next 3 hdc. 1 hdcfp around next hdcfp. *2 hdc in next hdc. 1 hdc in each of next 3 hdc. 1 hdcfp around next hdcfp. Rep from * around. Join with sl st to top of ch 2. 60 sts.

7th rnd: Ch 2. 1 hdc in same sp as last sl st. 1 hdc in each of next 4 hdc. 1 hdcfp around next hdcfp. *2 hdc in next hdc. 1 hdc in each of next 4 hdc. 1 hdcfp

around next hdcfp. Rep from * around. Join with sl st to top of ch 2. 70 sts.

8th rnd: Ch 2. 1 hdc in each of next 5 hdc. 1 hdcfp around next hdcfp. *1 hdc in each of next 6 hdc. 1 hdcfp around next hdcfp. Rep from * around. Join with sl st to top of ch 2.

Rep last rnd 7 times more.

Dec as follows:

1st rnd: Ch 1. Hdc in next hdc— beg dec made. 1 hdc in each of next 4 hdc. 1 hdcfp around next hdcfp. *Hdc2tog. 1 hdc in each of next 4 hdc. 1 hdcfp around next hdcfp. Rep from * around. Join with sl st to first st. 60 sts.

2nd rnd: Beg dec. 1 hdc in each of next 3 hdc. 1 hdcfp around next hdcfp. *Hdc2tog. 1 hdc in each of next 3 hdc. 1 hdcfp around next hdcfp. Rep from * around.

Join with sl st to first st. 50 sts. Insert ottoman.

3rd rnd: Beg dec. 1 hdc in each of next 2 hdc. 1 hdcfp around next hdcfp. *Hdc2tog. 1 hdc in each of next 2 hdc. 1 hdcfp around next hdcfp. Rep from * around. Join with sl st to first st. 40 sts.

4th rnd: Beg dec. 1 hdc in next hdc. 1 hdcfp around next hdcfp. *Hdc2tog. 1 hdc in next hdc. 1 hdcfp around next hdcfp. Rep from * around. Join with sl st to first st. 30 sts.

5th rnd: Beg dec. 1 hdcfp around next hdcfp. *Hdc2tog. 1 hdcfp around next hdcfp. Rep from * around. Join with sl st to first st. 20 sts.

6th rnd: Ch 1. 1 hdc in next st. *Hdc2tog. Rep from * around. Join with sl st to first st. 10 sts. Fasten off leaving a long end. Thread end through rem sts and fasten securely.•

Easy

MEASUREMENTS

Small Bowl

• Approx 5"/12.5cm in diameter

Medium Bowl

• Approx 6"/15cm in diameter

Large Bowl

• Approx 7"/18cm in diameter

MATERIALS

Yarn 5

Bernat® *Maker Home Dec*™, 8.8oz/250g balls, each approx 317yd/290m (cotton/nylon)

Small Bowl

• 1 ball in #11009 Cream (A and B)

Medium Bowl

• 1 ball in #11020 Pacific Varg (A)

• 1 ball in #11009 Cream (B)

Large Bowl

• 1 ball in #10468782 Steel Blue (A)

• 1 ball in #10468784 Cream (B)

Hook

Size G/6 (4mm) crochet hook, *or size needed to obtain gauge*

GAUGE

17 sc and 19 rows = 4"/10cm using size G/6 (4mm) hook.
TAKE TIME TO CHECK GAUGE.

STITCH GLOSSARY

Scbl Single crochet in back loop only of next stitch.

BOWL (All Sizes)

With A, ch 2.

1st rnd: 8 sc in 2nd ch from hook. Join with sl st to first sc. 8 sc.

2nd rnd: Ch 1. 2 sc in each sc around. Join with sl st to first sc. 16 sc.

3rd rnd: Ch 1. 2 sc in first sc. 1 sc in next sc. *2 sc in next sc. 1 sc in next sc. Rep from * around. Join with sl st to first sc. 24 sc.

4th rnd: Ch 1. 2 sc in first sc. 1 sc in each of next 2 sc. *2 sc in next sc. 1 sc in each of next 2 sc. Rep from * around. Join with sl st to first sc. 32 sc.

5th rnd: Ch 1. 2 sc in first sc. 1 sc in each of next 3 sc. *2 sc in next sc. 1 sc in each of next 3 sc. Rep from * around.Join with sl st to first sc. 40 sc.

6th rnd: Ch 1. 1 sc in first sc. 1 sc in next sc. 2 sc in next sc. *1 sc in each of next 4 sc. 2 sc in next sc. Rep from * to last 2 sc. 1 sc in each of last 2 sc. Join with sl st to first sc. 48 sc.

7th rnd: Ch 1. 2 sc in first sc. 1 sc in each of next 5 sc. *2 sc in next sc. 1 sc in each of next 5 sc. Rep from * around. Join with sl st to first sc. 56 sc.

8th rnd: Ch 1. 1 sc in first sc. 1 sc in each of next 2 sc. 2 sc in next sc. *1 sc in each of next 6 sc. 2 sc in next sc. Rep from * to last 3 sc. 1 sc in each of last 3 sc. Join with sl st to first sc. 64 sc.

Medium and Large Bowls Only

9th rnd: Ch 1. 2 sc in first sc. 1 sc in each of next 7 sc. *2 sc in next sc. 1 sc in each of next 7 sc. Rep from * around. Join with sl st to first sc. 72 sc.

10th rnd: Ch 1. 1 sc in first sc. 1 sc in each of next 3 sc. 2 sc in next sc. *1 sc in each of next 8 sc. 2 sc in next

sc. Rep from * to last 4 sc. 1 sc in each of last 4 sc. Join with sl st to first sc. 80 sc.

Large Bowl Only

11th rnd: Ch 1. *2 sc in next sc. 1 sc in each of next 9 sc. Rep from * around. Join with sl st to first sc. 88 sc.

12th rnd: Ch 1. 1 sc in first sc. 1 sc in each of next 4 sc. 2 sc in next sc. *1 sc in each of next 10 sc. 2 sc in next sc. Rep from * to last 5 sc. 1 sc in each of next 5 sc. Join with sl st to first sc. 96 sc.

All Sizes

Next rnd: Ch 1. 1 scbl in each sc around. Join with sl st to first sc.

Next rnd: Ch 1. 1 sc in each st around. Join with sl st to first sc. Rep last rnd 3 (4–5) times more.

Medium and Large Bowls Only

Break A. Join B.

All Sizes

Next rnd: Ch 1. 1 sc in each sc around. Join with sl st to first sc. Rep last rnd 2 (3-4) times more.

Next rnd: Ch 1. Working from left to right, instead of right to left as usual, work 1 reverse sc (see page 5) in each sc around. Join with sl st to first sc. Fasten off.•

CABLEWORK BLANKET

Intermediate

MEASUREMENTS
Approx 44"/112cm wide x 57"/145cm long

MATERIALS
Yarn (5)

Bernat® *Maker Home Dec*™, 8.8oz/250g balls, each approx 317yd/290m (cotton/nylon)
• 8 balls in #11008 Clay

Hook
• Size L/11 (8mm) crochet hook, *or size needed to obtain gauge*

GAUGE
10 sc and 11 rows = 4"/10 cm using size L/11 (8mm) hook. *TAKE TIME TO CHECK GAUGE.*

STITCH GLOSSARY
Dcfp Yoh and draw up a loop around post of indicated stitch, inserting hook from front to back to front. (Yoh and draw through 2 loops on hook) twice

Trfp Yoh twice and draw up a loop around post of indicated stitch, inserting hook from front to back to front. (Yoh and draw through 2 loops on hook) 3 times.

Cable Panel Pat (worked over 16 sts; see Diagram on page 64)

1st row: (RS) 1 sc in each of next 2 sc. (1 dcfp around post of next st 2 rows below) twice. 1 sc in each of next 2 sc. Skip next 2 sts. (1 trfp around post of next st 2 rows below) twice. *Working behind 2 trfp just made,* 1 trfp around post of each of 2 skipped sts 2 rows below. 1 sc in each of next 2 sc. (1 dcfp around post of next st 2 rows below) twice. 1 sc in each of next 2 sc.

2nd and alt rows: 1 sc in each of next 16 sts.

3rd row: 1 sc in each of next 2 sc. (1 dcfp around post of next st 2 rows below) twice. 1 sc in each of next 2 sc. (1 dcfp around post of next st 2 rows below) 4 times. 1 sc in each of next 2 sc. (1 dcfp around post of next st

2 rows below) twice. 1 sc in each of next 2 sc.

5th row: As 1st row.

7th row: 1 sc in each of next 3 sc. (1 trfp around post of next dcfp 2 rows below) twice. (1 trfp around post of next trfp 2 rows below) twice. 1 sc in each of next 2 sc. (1 trfp around post of next trfp 2 rows below) twice. (1 trfp around post of next dcfp 2 rows below) twice. 1 sc in each of next 3 sc.

9th row: 1 sc in each of next 3 sc. Skip next 2 sts. (1 trfp around post of next trfp 2 rows below) twice. Working behind 2 trfp just made, 1 trfp around post of each of 2 skipped sts 2 rows below. 1 sc in each of next 2 sc. Skip next 2 sts. (1 trfp around post of next trfp 2 rows below) twice. Working in front of 2 trfp just made, 1 trfp around post of each of 2 skipped sts 2 rows below.1 sc in each of next 3 sc.

11th row: 1 sc in each of next 2 sc. (1 trfp around post of next trfp 2 rows below) twice. 1 sc in each of next 2 sc. (1 trfp around post of next trfp 2 rows below) 4 times. 1 sc in each of next 2 sc. (1 trfp around post of next trfp 2 rows below) twice. 1 sc in each of next 2 sc.

13th row: As 3rd row.

14th row: As 2nd row. These 14 rows form Cable Panel Pat.

BLANKET (see Diagram on page 64)
Ch 120.

Set-up row 1: (WS) 1 dc in 4th ch from hook (counts as 2 dc). 1 dc in each ch to end of chain. Turn. 118 dc.

Set-up row 2: Ch 1. 1 sc in first dc. (1 dcfp around post of next dc) twice. 1 sc in each of next 3 dc. Ch 1. Skip next dc. *1 sc in each of next 4 dc. (1 dcfp around post of next dc) twice. 1 sc in each of next 2 dc. (1 dcfp around post of next dc) 4 times. 1 sc in each of next 2 dc. (1 dcfp around post of next dc) twice. 1 sc in each of next 4 dc. Ch 1. Skip next dc. Rep from * 4 times more. 1 sc in each of next 3 dc. (1 dcfp around post of next dc) twice. 1 sc in last dc. Turn.

Set-up row 3: Ch 1. 1 sc in each st and ch-1 sp to end

of row. Turn. Proceed in pat as follows:

1st row: (RS) Ch 1. 1 sc in first sc. (1 dcfp around post of next dcfp 2 rows below) twice. 1 sc in next sc. *Working in front of row, 1 tr in next skipped sc 2 rows below. Skip next sc (behind tr). 1 sc in next sc. Ch 1. Skip next sc. 1 sc in next sc. Working in front of row, 1 tr in same skipped sc 2 rows below as last tr. Skip next sc (behind tr).** Work 1st row of Cable Panel Pat across next 16 sc. Rep from * 4 times more, then from * to ** once. 1 sc in next sc. (1 dcfp around post of next dcfp 2 rows below) twice. 1 sc in last sc. Turn.

2nd row: Ch 1. 1 sc in each st and ch-1 sp to end of row. Turn.

These 2 rows form V Texture pat. Cable Panel Pat is now in position. Cont in pat (as placed in last rows) until Blanket measures approx 56½" [143.5 cm], ending on a 1st row of Cable Panel Pat.

Last row: (WS) Ch 3 (counts as dc). 1 dc in each st or ch-1 sp to end of row. Fasten off.

FINISHING

Fringe (see illustration on page 18)

Cut lengths of yarn 18"/45.5cm long. Taking 3 strands tog, knot into fringe evenly across each end of Blanket. Trim fringe evenly.•

CABLEWORK BLANKET

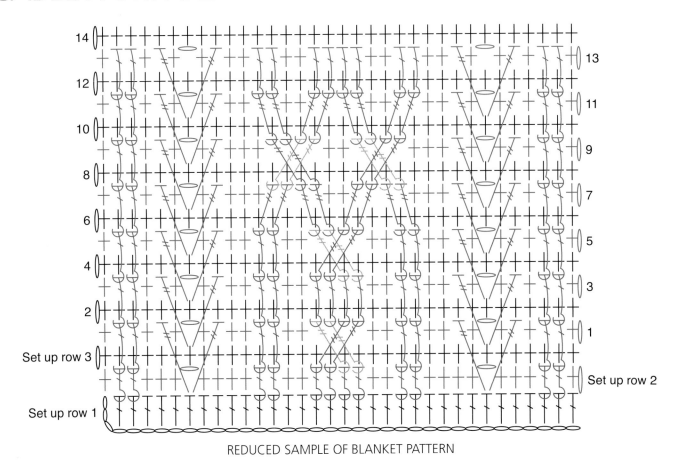

REDUCED SAMPLE OF BLANKET PATTERN

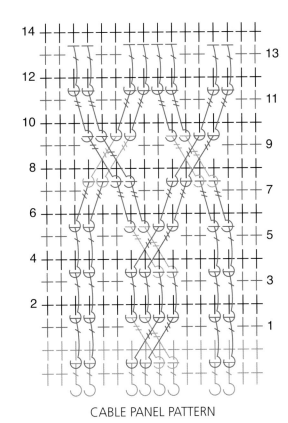

CABLE PANEL PATTERN

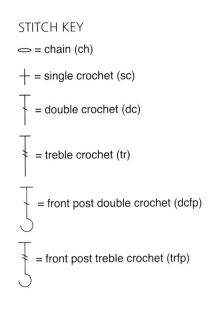

STITCH KEY

⬯ = chain (ch)

╀ = single crochet (sc)

┰ = double crochet (dc)

┱ = treble crochet (tr)

┦ = front post double crochet (dcfp)

┩ = front post treble crochet (trfp)